Off The Top of My Head

Off The Top of My Head

Adelaide S. McLeod

iUniverse, Inc.

New York Lincoln Shanghai

Off The Top of My Head

iUniverse books may be ordered through booksellers or by contacting:

iUniverse
2021 Pine Lake Road, Suite 100
Lincoln, NE 68512
www.iuniverse.com
1-800-Authors (1-800-288-4677)

Because of the dynamic nature of the Internet, any Web addresses or links contained in this book may have changed since publication and may no longer be valid.

The views expressed in this work are solely those of the author and do not necessarily reflect the views of the publisher, and the publisher hereby disclaims any responsibility for them.

ISBN: 978-0-595-44836-4 (pbk)
ISBN: 978-0-595-89156-6 (ebk)

Printed in the United States of America

Thank you, dear friends, who encouraged my writing, Dennis Held, editor extraordinaire, SMAGs, (Second Monday Writers' Group), my sounding board, husband Jack, my alter ego and my parents, C. J. and Sugar for giving me life.

Although I'm certifiably old, (I unabashedly admit to being a great-grandmother, an octogenarian, an old fossil), there is still a part of me that has never grown up. I find fairies, fantasy and magic irresistible. Of all my childhood books, my favorite stories came from the Arabian Nights.

Today, I went for groceries at Albertsons. As I approached the entrance, I whispered under my breath, "Open Sesame" and as the door swung open, I felt a surge of incredible power.

Contents

TRUST

The lake lolls in the silver serenity of October now that the speedboats and jet skis are in dry dock and the flatlanders have gone home. The ginnala maples have crimsoned, the aspen gather sunlight, as though they are compensating for the gray sky. The stillness of the crisp sweet air of the forest exudes a peace that doesn't exist in the valley below, where the anniversary of 9-11 still echoes though our city. Suspicion rides the winds of autumn, gathering hate.

An apartment building that housed refugee Islamic folk burned to the ground and in a different fire, little children lost their Islamic mother. Fear taints the air like that fire, sucking the oxygen leaving us gasping, unable to breathe. President Bush forges on against Saddam Hussein. Is there no end to it?

But here, on Payette Lake, there are no threats, no ugliness on this incredible day. Morning silence is only broken by a chipmunk jabbering, and a blue jay's "caw", as he swoops down for a remnant of our breakfast waffles. And there, on the deck that separates the cabin from the lake, a red fox is peeking in the window. His coat is russet silk; his spindly black legs seem too fragile to carry him.

I open the fridge, looking for his usual egg, but there aren't any so I dump a bag of pretzels on the deck as he watches me from a distance. He comes a little closer but then startles and runs as I stand up too abruptly. He clearly has little interest in the pretzels or the half banana I leave on the deck floor. He looks up, after sniffing them, as if to say, "Oh, come on, lady, you can do better than that."

So I take a chicken breast out of the freezer and defrost it in the microwave while he patiently waits and watches. He is cautious and so am I as I kneel to his level. He comes hesitantly and takes the chicken out of my hand. He stands right there, nonchalantly chomping on it until it is gone. Then, he curls up on the bench just a few feet away for a little nap. I feel elation that I can't explain.

My mind drifts back to the other world to which I must return. And I wonder, what will it take to build such a bridge of trust between men, between countries?

GOING TO THE DOGS

After reaching that scary plateau, where much of our social life had become attending funerals of our friends, Jack and I realized we were over-the-hill and tumbling full-speed down the other side. Thinking we'd better do something about it, we read everything available about longevity.

Our research revealed there are many things you must do if you expect to stay alive: walk a mile every day, limit cholesterol intake, drink a glass of red wine with dinner, eat colorful food such as spinach, broccoli, salmon, and tomatoes, and take the entire alphabet of vitamins. Health gurus expound on going to bed early, sleeping eight hours, praying a lot, meditating, exercising, and staying cheerful. We've done it all and it seemed to work as neither of us has shown up on the obituary page.

Then, I read an article that literally changed our lives. The author professed that people who own pets live longer. Now, where is the logic in that? I didn't have a clue, but at our age, we couldn't afford to pass up any possible advantage, so I ran right out and bought a dog, a very big dog. I figured that if a dog would make us live longer, a big dog should keep blood flowing in our veins for years to come.

Jack was skeptical. "Dogs are a big expense and a lot of work," he said. Yet after he met Dutch (short for Duchess), a beautiful seven-month-old female German shepherd, who cocked her head and smiled at him, he caved in.

Adjustments come hard at our age. We hadn't realized how set in our ways we had become. We were accustomed to spending our first two hours every morning luxuriating over a cappuccino, waking up slowly, reading the morning paper, and perhaps a chapter or two in a good novel. We were soon to discover there would be no more lounging. Before Dutch, I seldom dressed before ten, but what would the neighbors think if I chased my dog through their delphiniums in my night-gown? Now, I am up and dressed and lucky to get a quick sip of coffee before Her Highness barks to go outside. It is still dark at six a. m. While I hold her leash, Dutch decides whether or not she is going to "do it."

Once back in the house, she barks for her breakfast but she refuses to eat Purina's best without a little embellishment. While she's eating, I take a short hiatus to look at the front page of the paper, or brush my teeth, but never have time for both. My old modus operandi, procrastination, is kaput.

Once Dutch finishes eating, she wants her walk. She prances around, acting nervous, giving us an emphatic message that she can't wait. We rush to get ourselves in gear, take her by the leash and head out the door and down the path that separates the river from the golf course. There is absolutely nothing else that could get the two of us "going" on a rainy morning like this poopy puppy has. For the next forty-five minutes, we walk the dog until we find a place where she can go safely off her leash. She loves to run. She plays a game with us and we have to do a little running ourselves before we get her back in our control. I have wanted to get Jack out of low gear for a long time, but never succeeded. Now, he is running at a full gallop trying to head off Dutch at the pass. Jack is looking younger already.

While caring for Dutch's needs, there is nothing that can make one feel quite so ridiculous as holding a leash while the dog attached to the other end goes potty. There is a trick to it: I divert my eyes toward the sky and act as though this dog isn't mine. Then, I take the Mutt Mitt and dispose of the leavings after *it* happens. Through two plies of plastic, I pick up the dog's calling card with my hand and then turn the bag inside out and tie a knot in it to carry it home where I toss it in the garbage as nonchalantly as possible. Not in my most bizarre dreams did I imagine I'd be doing something so disgusting.

When we finally arrive home, Dutch takes a nap while we clean up her window smudges, dog hair and paw prints. Every day, I find myself down on my hands and knees wiping doggie "mistakes" out of the white carpet. But what do I care? That is a small price to pay for guaranteed longevity.

Suddenly, it is deja-vu. This is like raising kids all over again, I think; except most kids don't shed. And, then I think about how I could have spent the morning reading a good book.

The afternoon repeats the morning but might include a trip to the Hair of the Dog, a doggie beauty parlor, for a wash and blow dry, or a trip to Petco for another new leash. Dutch manages to chew them up as fast as I buy them. While I am there I get a sack of doggie treats. There are occasional trips to the grocery for dog bones—at $5.00 a pop; in the good old days, dog bones were free.

There's this thing about the odor. I complained to my vet, "Dutch smells *doggy*." The vet gives me a bemused look and says, "Well, she is a dog, isn't she?" Then, she gets serious: "Weekly baths might help."

So off I go to the Puppy Parlor and $55.00 later, Dutch smells a whole lot better. However, the smell returns after a day or two, so I resort to the do-it-yourself

Doggie Do for half the price. I put on my sweats, take the dog by the leash and off we go. The whole ordeal is a humongous struggle. Dutch has no desire to get into the bathtub; once she is in she doesn't want to get out. After a couple of hours, we walk out together. Dutch is clean, blown dry, and looking beautiful. I am soggy wet, exhausted and smell like a dog.

While we are still adjusting to sharing our domicile with this hairy creature, she goes into heat. Jack and I are very private people when it comes to our personal hygiene. Jack never fails to close the bathroom door, even though we are the only two in the house. I am slightly worse. So picture this overly modest couple wrestling 60-pound hyper-pup in the parking lot of Petco trying to put a doggie Kotex on her. I keep looking out of the corner of my eye expecting someone I know to show up, and sure enough, here come the Johnsons. I blush and try to make small talk but the Johnsons won't quit laughing.

I make a desperate call to the Vet who says to bring Dutch in and have her spayed. When we pick her up a couple of days later, she is glad to see us but is suffering post-op depression. She mopes around the house and won't eat.

We considered getting her a shrink. Instead, I start adding Marie Callenders' $2.48 a can soup to her daily diet. The dog loves it; now there is no way to stop giving it to her.

When people get as old as Jack and I are, they seem to get less flexible. We move slower and everything takes longer. But thanks to our longevity program, I'm am able to drag myself out of bed at two o'clock in the morning, to stand in my nightie in the front yard and freeze my tush. By this time, I don't care what the neighbors think.

We find ourselves walking Dutch rain or shine, morning and night. She is a handful and has the strength of a bulldozer. I find myself running to keep up; I find myself in a heap on the grass when the dog bolts. As Jack picks me up, I think, "Hallelujah! That must have added at least five years to my life."

Since Dutch has bonded with us, she has become very possessive. She guards us from our grandchildren when they drop by. Her barks and growls make them leery of her. Jack gives them some of those little doggies biscuits to buy her affection, but she isn't interested in such meager offerings. Korie, our granddaughter finds a tenderloin in the frig that was going to be our supper. Every dog has its price; that is hers.

Before long, we decide we need an invisible fence to keep Dutch in the yard. Eleven hundred and seventy five dollars later, the fence is installed; more than three times what we paid for the darn dog. The installer demonstrates how it works. We are procrastinating. It's just too hard to listen to Dutch yelp when she gets shocked. But it would be nice to be able to let her out the door now and then and know she won't get in trouble with the neighbors or worse yet, end up in the clink. So our plan is to go about it slowly and make it work. Maybe sometime late next summer—or not.

Jack bought Dutch a "Gentle Leader" with the hope it would make her easier to control. It is a contraption like a hackamore used on a horse. The theory is the dog doesn't like pressure on the nose and won't fight against the leash. The problem is, no one told Dutch about this theory. She leaps like a jackrabbit, wallows on the grass, digs her snout in the dirt and does flip-flops: she hates it.

Finally we admit the dog is totally out of control and realize that something must be done: we enroll her in Obedience School. With our luck, she'll likely have us trained in no time. Something has to happen because we are both weary of having our shoulders dislocated when we walk her. I don't mind falling occasionally—I do it gracefully, I even bounce—but it is a bit embarrassing when I land in the middle of a mud puddle in front of a group of golfers.

No question, we're in this for the long haul. Sooner or later we may get smarter than the dog. In the meantime, we're not sorry Dutch came into our lives. Sure, she's a house-wrecker, but she's added a nice dimension to our family and we *are* more physically active.

Indeed, taking on a dog has been a crossroad in our lives; she changed everything. If it wasn't for her, we might have succumbed to living in the past where rocking-chair conversation would drift to memories of a dog we owned forty years ago instead of the rigorous here-and-now life we've found with Dutch. Besides, I wouldn't have such a good argument for buying new carpeting.

Live longer? We'll have to. This darn dog with her expensive tastes is counting on us for support. No one else would understand about the Marie Callender thing, or put up with a dozen chewed-up leashes. Besides, I can't overlook what a delicious treat it is to stand out in the refreshing midnight air while the sweet thing runs circles around me deciding whether or not she is going to piddle.

I have to go now. Jack is waiting in the car. I'm driving him to Emergency to have his shoulder set. We'll settle for whatever it takes. Neither of us is ready to concede that our shelf life has expired or we've passed our expiration date.

THE ALLEY

I love every grain of its coarse orange sand, this gathering place of my childhood where I learned the difference between democracy and despotism. In this "no-man's land" the thirteen kids on our block, in a wide spread of ages, developed our notion of civility as we sparred for our niche in the whole. Righteousness prevailed, even though it might have been multifarious and slow. Bullies were among us but not for long. It was where I went to look for the Bobbies and the Bettys in my world.

Our thirteen came from principled, stoic, no-nonsense parents who, from the cradle up, fed us virtue as surely as they fed us food. Dependably solid, they taught us love without hugging or repeating that daily liturgy, "I love you."

As I learned to play hopscotch, marbles, run sheep run, and kick the can; I learned the basic rules for getting along in this world. I learned about the give and take of sharing, and what it took to be a friend. No, things weren't always fair, but nothing in this world is, and that may have been the biggest lesson of all. This alley was an intriguing place with endless possibilities where I was never bored or had thoughts of leaving until my mother's whistle called me home.

I feel sorry for children who have no alley, no neutral ground in which to experiment, to discover how human relations work. In my alley, there were no adults to muddle up progress, to stifle our discoveries; we were compelled to create our own society. Such freedom doesn't exist on school playgrounds or in Little League, where adults rule.

From this alley and others like it across the country came what Tom Brokaw dubbed the "Greatest Generation." What did we have besides the Depression and World War II? We had outstanding parents and we had alleys.

THE TURTLE PEOPLE

Now, I'm pretty broad-minded. Ask anyone. I adhere to the code of "live and let live" and applaud human differences whatever they may be. Diversity makes life fascinating. This pertains to people in all walks of life with the exception of serial killers and primadonnas

Knowing I am going to step on some toes here, I have to say, I have a real beef with one other sector of our society, the Turtle People. They need to be reckoned with as they are rapidly taking over the highways and ruining my peace of mind.

Turtle People are peculiar. I'm no psychologist but I keenly feel that they suffer from an attachment syndrome. When they get ready to go on a week's vacation, they don't simply get in their cars like the rest of us do and go. They load up everything they own like food, clothing, bicycles, fishing gear, lawn chairs, rubber boats, water skis, swim fins and all fourteen volumes of the Encyclopedia Britannica, and pack it into a huge white box with a motor in the front. This rig is so big you could put a dozen VW Bugs inside and still sleep eight. It seems like the Turtle People's greatest fear is leaving anything, anything at all, behind. This is a pretty telling sign of phobic behavior if you ask me.

Once the big white box is loaded as tight as Kristie Ally stuffed into a size six dress, they still aren't satisfied. They attach a trailer behind it so they can take whatever wouldn't fit inside the big white box. Then their paranoia drives them to take their automobile along. They've taken everything else so why not? On its own little trailer, they hook it to the back of the first trailer. And just when we think they have appeased their dementia they attach their 20-foot motorboat behind that. And we watch as we expect them to load at least five or six kids into the big white box but no, it is just the two of them.

They look like a train, a long train, as they roll out of their subdivision and down the road. Now this is where things get troublesome. They get out on the highway, not just any highway—they pick the narrow roads that are mountainous and winding.

Going up steep grades, the best they can do is seven miles per hour as their motor is too small and their load too heavy. They take up their side of the road and ours as well and we are stuck behind them. They are a hundred-foot-long menace and so tall they block the daylight; there is no way to see around them. How are we ever going to pass them?

Finally, out of desperation we risk it because we need to arrive at our destination before it is time to go back home. Once around them, we discover their clone ahead of us and then, their clone and their clone. This is madness, lunacy, craziness. It is not fair to those of us who are certifiably sane. There should be a law against Turtle People. No big white monstrosity should be allowed to give us ulcers, to drag all of the TP's obsessions behind it. Nor should they be allowed on narrow roads or in heavy traffic and cause a catastrophe.

I'm going to email my Senator, maybe even the President, write a letter to the Editor and start a petition. I propose we keep the Turtle People off our highways. In all fairness, they *could* be allowed when the traffic isn't so heavy—say mid-week, every other Wednesday, between two and four in the morning.

DEATH OF A LANDMARK

After spending Christmas of 1950 with our respective families in Boise, Jack and I were on our way back to the wilds of Montana where Jack was an engineer on the Hungry Horse Dam and I was the receptionist in the project office. We climbed the depot hill in our new-to-us 1939 Chevy and turned left on the old Mountain Home Highway. Where the highway hugged the edge of the bench, I craned my neck for one last look at our hometown. Going away to college hadn't bothered me much because I knew I would be going back home; this was different. We had been gone from Boise for more than a year, yet it wasn't until this cold day in January that it hit me.

Boise was the small town where my roots grew deep. Our white bungalow on the corner of East Washington and Locust Streets had been the only home I had ever known. I was born in the front bedroom; our wedding reception was held in its garden.

Home for the holidays, we frantically spent our days seeking out familiar landmarks and faces, trying to stir memories and bring pieces of our discarded childhoods into focus. Boise was a pretty town with tree-lined streets where the faces you passed walking down the sidewalk were most always familiar. On the surface, my parents seemed unchanged, yet it was strange to feel like a guest in their home.

After college, our friends scattered. Only a handful remained in Boise, but there were others, like us, who were "home" for the holidays. There was always a formal party or two at Christmas time, so we came prepared. The two most stylish venues were the elegant Crystal Ballroom in the Boise Hotel and the Grand Ballroom in the Elks Lodge on 9th and Jefferson. It was always a thrill to dine and dance to live music and visit with old friends. The lagoon at Julia Davis Park has frozen over that year, so we dug out our old ice skates. We visited the parents of our closest friends and, of course, found time to pop in to say hello to our old neighbors and favorite teachers.

In this river valley cupped in sagebrush foothills, palatial houses graced Warm Springs Avenue and Harrison Boulevard. Masonry edifices embellished with corbelled brick, Roman arched sandstone, Ionic pillars, ponderous brass doors and temperamental elevators made up the downtown.

The imposing sandstone State Capitol building with its porte-cocheres, cold gray marble rotunda, dome and sky-lit senate was a rendition of our nation's Capitol Building.

The town boasted three hotels. The Idan-ha, the oldest, was a dilapidated relic. But, its jutting corner turret enhanced the streetscape. The Owyhee exuded old-world elegance. In the lobby, an army of mohair davenports stood stiffly on lush oriental carpets in a most splendid way. Hotel Boise, the town's salute to Art Deco, was built just before the 1929 "Crash" and housed Boise's only penthouse.

Downtown Boise had five theaters: the Pinney, the Fox (originally the Egyptian), Granada, Rialto and Rio. The Pinney was the grandest, with its loge seats on the mezzanine, its upper balcony and layer upon layer of maroon velvet curtains. The Fox (Egyptian) reflected treasures of King Tut's tomb with exotic hieroglyphics on pillared walls. The Sphinx-faced animals sitting on their haunches with dangling naked breasts insulted my modesty.

The tearoom of the Mode Department Store was the place mothers took their daughters to test their table manners, where twenty-five cent allowances bought a grilled tuna sandwich and a Coke and left you ten cents for admission into the Saturday Matinée to see Roy Rogers.

Every spring, our mothers marched us in to The Mode to buy white dress shoes and Easter bonnets that Mrs. Chapman, the owner, brought back from the New York market. Boise was a great place to grow up.

On our last evening, we strolled downtown window-shopping. We stopped for a marshmallow Coke at Tillotsons, kitty-corner from the post office. Back out on the street, we walked south on Eighth Street. On the south-east corner of Eighth and Idaho Streets, I expected to see the City Hall. My heart sank as I realized the Boise's most cherished landmark was missing. The heart and soul of the city was gone. I stood there reconstructing in my mind just how it looked. It came easy because I had always been impressed by it: Romanesque in style, five-stories tall, with imaginative neo-classic overtones. Under quaint turrets, stairways wound beneath and above continuous curved arches. Stone steps were concave from years of comings and goings of Boise's town folk.

I felt betrayed. An important part of our city's past had been decimated, pulverized and hauled away. Where the City Hall once stood, a ghastly common box-like structure loomed. A neon sign read "Walgreen's Drug Store." The gigantic bowl-shaped water fountain in front of the City Hall was gone too. It had been a gathering spot in our school days. Who was responsible? How could Boise's town folk stand by and let this happen?

Our holiday came to an end. The New Year was upon us and it was time to go back to our other world. By the time we reached Mountain Home, my thoughts were caught up in all-consuming nostalgia. How painful it was to have the most outstanding landmark of my hometown destroyed. How hard to dismiss the past and let it disappear. As we turned north out of Mountain Home, headed for Salmon, and then on to Montana, it hit me.

The old City Hall and my childhood were gone for good. There would be no going back to what once was.

I turned in my seat and looked ahead at the long winding road of an unknown future and wondered what it would hold. I felt a stir of excitement muddled with anxiety. Jack and I were setting out to establish our own family, now. That was the way it should be. And I wondered, would it all be this hard?

KEEPERS

In every home, there's a drawer that collects things you are somehow compelled to keep but you're not sure why: stray paper clips, an "I Like Ike" campaign button, a pebble you carried back from your trek into the Sawtooth Mountains, the pamphlet a man wearing a black suit and a gray face thrust on you at the funeral that summed up your friend's life in two paragraphs.

Then there is a lone gray button that came off a jacket you had almost forgotten you ever owned, a jelly bean that has grown fur, three quarters with new images depicting Delaware, New Hampshire and Rhode Island, a thirty-two-cent stamp that your Scottish thrift won't allow you to throw away, and a match book from the Eiffel Tower Dining Room. You know you are dealing with a compulsion here. This drawer is the refuge last resort for the misfits, the orphans of your domicile, a conundrum like a dirty little secret you wouldn't want your neighbors to know about. It is particularly annoying, as you subscribe to the axiom: "A place for everything and everything in its place."

Some day, you could by chance open this drawer, and if you do, you just might happen to pick up the pebble that traveled in your pocket up the trails of the Sawtooth Mountains and if you rub it in your fingers for a minute or two, it might spark a memory of a pristine lake embellished with pines when you cast your fly out on mirror-like water and caught a 10-inch rainbow trout that you roasted on a stick over a campfire like a marshmallow. A meadow, there, ran wild with blue camas and you saw a perfect doe grazing on the tender grass with her spotted, new-born fawn. And you might remember that when you were exhausted from the long climb, your resourceful sons pushed you from behind up the last rise of the mountain like you were an old jalopy out of gas.

Standing over your junk drawer, you toss the pebble back where you found it as you seriously consider dumping the whole messy plethora of stuff into the trash. Yet, some time in the future, something in that drawer could conjure up a pleasant memory. Maybe that justifies keeping it, and then again, maybe not.

MESSAGE FROM MARS

Almost overnight, married life with Brian has turned into a travesty, and you can't see any way to fix it. And to think it's all because you are writing a story on your new computer. Sunday morning, up at five, you watch daybreak's pink chiffon cover the sky, the mountains, the river, as your fingers pound the computer keys. You have learned to merge, save, copy, spell check and give up eating.

You are writing a fantasy, a terrestrial tale set on the tiny plant of Futura that lies somewhere in the solar system between Jupiter and Mars, which, environmentally is ten million light years ahead of Earth. Futura abounds with humans, flora and fauna who all speak the same language and live in harmony, an enchanting place that overflows with magic and mystery.

You name your heroine Serena. Serena comes to life so quickly, so effortlessly, it is as though she creates herself, like she's always been there waiting. An Aquarius born on a full moon with an Aires rising, she is marvelously seductive—her green eyes glitter like the stars. She smiles and her rosebud lips kiss the air. Corn silk hair flowing wildly to her waist is strewn with violets, stardust, song birds and butterflies. Mushroom-soft skin befits this stunning creature of nature. As she whispers musical incantations, her graceful fingers cast their spell. Men, mesmerized by her charm, are transported to the celestial clouds of insatiable desire.

This same Sunday morning, you hand Brian your first few pages with his coffee and you wait while he reads them—and rereads them. He looks at you. "I had no idea you had such thoughts," he says. "I'll be ... this is good, really good. I like your character Serena, like her a lot."

"Of course, I have thoughts like this," you mumble under your breath. "You just never seem to notice." Sometimes you wonder if he really knows you at all. Yet the fact that he likes your story sends you scurrying back to the computer to write more.

Out of bed before dawn, in your worn-out bathrobe with yesterday's mascara on your cheeks you plug away until noon, one, two in the afternoon. Staring into the monitor, you realize you are obsessed; you are a helpless appendage of your computer. You are in its spell and doing its bidding.

As Serena becomes ever more desirable, you become more of a slob. You begin to resent any intrusion so you unplug the telephone and quit answering the doorbell. Brian indulges you; it is not like him. He brings you small morsels of food, coffee. He waits at your elbow for the next chapter. Brain talks about Serena as though she is a house guest. You get a strange feeling that he likes her too much. She is younger, prettier, more mysterious and sexier.

Without any warning, your screen goes blank. Your 122 pages disappear into the computer's dark recesses for no reason at all. You fear they will never surface again. The desire to throw your paper weight through the monitor is overwhelming. You feel yourself teetering off the edge of sanity.

Even so, you aren't prepared for Brian's reaction when you tell him what has happened. He yells at you: "How could you be so careless. This is homicide. Get her back."

You try everything you can think of and finally resort to reading the manual. At the bottom of Page 1008 you realize you haven't understood one word. In desperation, you call your savvy computer guru. A hundred dollars later, he pulls up some gobbledygook. "This is your file," he says. "It's scrambled with some other stuff."

It looks like a message from Mars: Cs with little beards, square boxes and Os wearing beanies. You spend days deleting the garbage until finally Serena reappears, unscathed. You celebrate by going out to dinner. Brian makes a reservation for three.

That night, Brian mumbles in his sleep, "Serena, Serena." At that moment you realize you are playing second fiddle to this sexy trollop. You think about covering Brian's face with a pillow but instead, you settle for pulling off his covers.

Brian leaves home early the next morning and when he comes back after dark, he is driving a brand new Porsche, wearing a neon Spandex shirt; his graying hair has been touched up. He looks cool, but you worry that it's not you he is trying to impress. Brian takes your latest chapter and goes into the den to read it. You hear him giggling; you hear musical laughter. There is no mistaking it—it's Serena. You jump up from your computer and peek around the corner.

There Serena is, doing that sensuous thing with her hands and flashing her eyes at Brian. He is enjoying it far too much. Are you losing your mind? In desperation, you run out of the house. The stars wink at you; they know what is going on. The moon glares at you in disgust. You feel light headed. "Get a grip," you mumble to yourself. Taking a deep breath, clenching your teeth, you tiptoe into the house and peek into the den. Brain is sleeping; he has that grin on his face; he is alone.

Back at the computer, you give Serena a heinous wart on her nose. Not quite satisfied, you add a grotesque hair growing out of it. You delete her musical laughter and give her a cackle.

The next morning you hand Brian a new Serena in the next chapter.

"Thank God," Brian says. "She was too perfect. She's more human this way."

Rats! Why did you show him your story in the first place? Frazzled, you can't think. Too many hours at the computer makes your eyes work like burned-out flash bulbs. You need sleep.

At the crack of dawn, the sun dances off the raindrops on the windowpane and you feel better. Today, you will do something drastic.

As you open the kitchen cupboard for a bag of coffee beans, a mouse flies in your face. You panic as its claws dig into your leg as it scampers to the floor and disappears while you finish your scream. Espresso! You need espresso and you need it strong. You pour a cup and belt it down and pour a second.

Something is crawling all over your body. You rip off your bathrobe to discover an army of spiders trying to devour you. You jump, you stomp, you slap your body red.

As you watch a squirrel in the glass cookie jar finish the last biscotti, you realize you are standing in the kitchen buff-naked. Dashing to your bedroom, you hide under the covers and lie in a quiet shiver, in the fetal position, desperately trying to disappear into a womb of calm; the walls echo your pitiful whimpering.

Someone is sitting on your bed, tugging at your covers. You peek out to see her. "Serena," you whine, "How could you?" Get your wild life out of my house ... please."

"All right, I will but only if you say you're sorry. You shouldn't have given me this yucky wart. That wasn't fair."

"What's fair about seducing my husband?"

"Oh, that. You made me the way I am, you know."

"Serena, get back into the computer now and behave yourself."

"Why should I? I'm a figment of your imagination; you've given me mystical powers and I intend to use them." Serena cackles as she evaporates into a puff of lavender smoke.

You spend the day under the covers, peeking out now and again hoping Serena's menagerie is gone. Writers sometimes do their best thinking with their heads under the covers, with their knees drawn up to their chins; you are no exception. Ideas begin to flow like rare wine into your goblet of inspiration.

Basking in the sunrise, you are in control. Exciting words flow onto the screen as you create Marcus, a sorcerer with incredible powers. He resembles Mars, the Roman god, but he is sensitive, a poet and has Mel Gibson's blue eyes. He calls Serena his Venus. He wills her to fall in love with him. She complies and they fly off together, through popcorn clouds, beyond the rainbow and out where the sky is always sapphire. They live happily ever after on the planet of Futura doing what lovers do.

You hand Brian the finished story and he reads it and then rereads it. There is no expression on his face and you can see he is deep in thought. Finally, he puts it down and looks at you. "You know, Angel, this is a terrific story. You're a darn good writer. I'm proud of you."

"What?" you gasp.

"Why wouldn't I be?"

"Are you aware I put an end to Serena? You seem so caught up in her."

"Oh, no I'm not," he laughs. "I was having fun. Once I figured out you were getting jealous of your own character, I just couldn't resist egging you on. I'll admit I played it for all it was worth. I even mumbled her name when you thought I was asleep."

"Then, you don't have a thing for Serena?"

"Of course not. You're my one and only."

"You know, Brain, I am getting pretty savvy on the computer. I could have deleted you with a click of the right button."

"You wouldn't do that."

"Better watch your step." You smile as your rosebud lips kiss the air.

Brain takes you in his arms and gives you a kiss that is off the charts. You whisper musical incantations in his ear as your graceful fingers cast their spell. Brian, mesmerized by your charm, is transported to the celestial clouds of insatiable desire.

MS. JUSTICE

There she stands in her nightgown, the blindfold of impartiality covering her eyes as she holds the scale of justice balanced in her right hand, the sword of power clenched in her left.

Weighing the two side of an argument is the business of jurisprudence. We are taught to believe truth in our court system will prevail—justice will persevere. That is how our forefathers, men of virtue, thought of it; but lately, the world has changed.

Maneuvering and manipulation has become a substitute for truth. Now our courts system seems to defer to whoever has the most money to buy the "sharkiest" lawyer. Haven't you ever wondered how a plea bargain can make a guilty person less guilty and more easily pardoned? The ideals that promote justice, fairness, righteousness and rectitude have been glossed over by chicanery until these principles we once lived by are all but forgotten.

Our lady, Ms. Justice, needs to pull off her blindfold and see what has happened to our court system. She needs to get out of her nightgown and put on her work clothes and get vocal. If she shouts loud enough she can wake up the silent majority. Unless she does, the scales of justice will never find true balance again.

SELECTED MEMORIES

Winding through the rawhide mountains north of Boise on Highway 55, into the Payette River canyon, passed Horse Shoe Bend and Gardena where the ponderosa pines begin to appear and the white water quickens, I suddenly have an overwhelming desire to make a U-turn and go back to the bridge at Gardena. There are no cars coming; my foot is on the brake; I turn the car around.

Many times on my way north, I have looked across the Payette at the old ranch, but never before had I seriously considered driving up the old cow-path road that I traveled so many times as a child in the back seat of my parents' 1931 Chrysler. My grandparents homesteaded this land at the turn of the century, and I spent many summers of my childhood with them.

Driving north to the cabin, I glance across the river from time-to-time. My anger grows in direct proportion to the neglect of the old homestead. Some time ago the barn burned down but worse: Grandma's yellow roses that trellised the garden gate are no more. The orchard and vineyard live only in memory. This oasis in the dry hills, fed by stream water where Gramps had planted locust, maple, mulberry, peach and cherry trees, where he had carved out a paradise, is strewn with abandoned trucks and farm machinery. The old ranch house, turned silver, stands ghost-like; its blank windows stare like mindless eyes. The porch hangs asunder.

I have often wondered about Billy Watson, the man whose grandfather bought this place from my grandfather more than sixty-five years ago. Why does he keep so much junk? I stop at the gate to read the sign: **No Trespassing—Private Property—Guard Dogs on Duty**. I slam the stick of my Beemer into low to maneuver the rutted road. Grabbing the steering wheel with a bit of rage that isn't often like me, I let out the clutch.

A few hundred yards ahead, up the hillside, sits a mobile home—probably where he lives. Right in front of my car, at the edge of the parking area, stands a downtown Boise parking meter, likely a trophy from some Saturday night escapade. I walk up a few wooden steps and knock on the door. Two blond teenage girls smile at me. "Pa's up at the old place," one of them says.

"Would it be all right for me to drive on in? I used to come here, as a child." They smile again and nod. Pretty nice daughters for a junker, I think. I navigate from pothole to puddle. To the right, on a fence post, sits an antique nickel cash register—the mechanical kind. A hundred yards down the road, on the left, a triangular Conoco sign rises twenty feet in the air with nothing but dry grass around it. At the top of the rise I get a panoramic view of the whole ranch. I want to cry.

As I drive down the narrow winding road, the fear of finally meeting Billy Watson consumes me. Three blue-eyed Australian Dingoes bark me into a place where I can see a couple of men working on an old truck. I stop the car. Their heads are bent intently under the raised hood and they don't look up from what they are doing. I take a deep breath, swallow hard and get out of the car in spite of the barking dogs. I stand there shaking inside and feeling invisible. I clear my throat, but that doesn't help. "Hello," I say as I inch toward them.

"Hello." One of the men finally acknowledges me. He is a nice looking man, whiskered yet neat and clean in his outdoor clothes. Billy Watson—and he is not as I had pictured him in my mind all these years. I tell him my grandparents homesteaded this place about a hundred years ago and ask if I can look around.

"Help yourself." He shrugs. Then, "I guess you're saying J. F. Thompson was your grandpa? Well, I'll be. The creek over yonder is named after him. We call it the J. F. Thompson Creek. It flows water year-round when all the others run dry. Some engineering, I'd say. He must have been a pretty smart fella."

"He was." It's nice to know my grandfather's name is still tied to the old homestead.

Billy puts his head back into the engine of the truck as I turn and walk toward the house. The back-porch, where the cream separator once stood, is littered with old magazines, tin cans and an unplumbed toilet. The screen door looks familiar; I pull it open just to hear it bang wondering if the sound will be familiar; it is.

Up behind the house stand the caved-in remains of the ice house with its thick walls filled with sawdust where sides of bacon and quarters of beef hung from rafters above blocks of ice. Gramps had cut that ice from the frozen river and pulled it up the riverbank with a team of horses.

The machine shop where everything had been so neatly hung on the walls, is still there. I remember a big flint sharpening wheel with pedals like a bicycle where I sat and pedaled so Gramps could sharpen his shovels and other tools, but it is gone. The creek ribbons though the locust trees and widens before it hurries down to the river just as it did so many years ago. The vineyard and orchard are gone and so is the big silver maple tree that held my swing.

Inside the house, the rooms are claustrophobic, nothing at all like I remember them. It is depressing so I go back outside. The land still sweeps majestically on this level shelf between the mountains and the Payette River.

I ride Old Blue along the meandering river bank watching Gramps fishing in the river. When his creel is full of salmon, he hops on Old Blue behind me and I give him a ride up to the kitchen door. Grandma fries the fish in her cast iron skillet in a little lard and we have them for breakfast. I follow Gramps down to the milk-shed where he squirts steaming milk into my mouth from a cow's teat.

I'm eye-to-eye with a flock of turkeys. Their beady red eyes scare me into covering my own eyes and I run blindly through them to my grandma's arms.

I sit in the crotch of a cherry tree as the big ripe Bings ping into my lard bucket and I vow to only eat every tenth one. I squat at the creek as my hollyhock dolls waltz in the swirling water. On a piece of bark, I send caterpillars that have fallen out of the mulberry tree on a fast ride to certain doom in the direction of the chicken house.

Out in the vegetable garden, Grandma and I dig potatoes the size of marbles to cream with her peas. "Darling little potatoes," we always call them. Under the fire-box of the Majestic Range squirms a litter of kittens that can't open their eyes yet. Sunflowers I picked for my grandma stand in a fruit jar on the table. The pattern has grown faint on the linoleum floor from so many scrubbings. The starched curtains hang between two nails on a piece of string. The wind up window blinds flutter if you pull on them just so. How soft the feather bed is that I share with my grandma.

The Edison phonograph plays Caruso; Gramps puts on a Scottish reel and I dance for him. He claps his hands and stamps his foot in time with the music; the pungent odor of his pipe; the aroma of Grandma's lamb stew; the soft glow of the coal-oil lamp after the sun goes down; the spicy scent when the wind blows north from the mint field; the two-hole outhouse where you can't flush; the smell of fresh-baked sourdough biscuits before I open my eyes in the morning; the fragrance of locust blossoms through the open window; the hole in the kitchen ceiling where Uncle Fred shot his "unloaded" rifle; the delicious fried chicken that Grandma serves on Sundays; chicken she won't eat because the chickens are her pets; the fainting couch where no one sits for long as it's stuffed with horsehair and is hard as a rock, but there isn't much sitting around time anyway.

I startled. Billy Watson stands at my elbow looking at me. In my excitement, I blurt, "Have you ever thought of selling?"

His eyes tear a little. "Someone wanted to buy the place once before. I knew he had the money. It made me feel kind of sick. I don't know where I'd go. I'd rather wrestle a loco bull than try to drive in that traffic down in Boise. My grandpa raised me here. I grew up in that house, lived with my grandpa, just him and me, and when he died my aunt and uncle moved in for a spell."

Wishing I'd kept my mouth shut, I say, "I understand."

"My clutter," he says, throwing his arms out to indicate the cars and machinery strewn about, "drives my wife nuts. But it's sort of my hobby. Some of it just getting good, I think. I may have to end up burying it. I can always dig it up later. Did you see my beach? Come on, I'll show you."

"I don't remember a beach," I say.

We walk along together and he tells me how they let their hogs run against the river. "The folks in that restaurant across the river had a big barbecue. The smell of it got to the pigs. They swum the river and caused a traffic jam on Highway 55. Didn't know hogs could swim until they did that."

"Another time, we were going to have a picnic down at our beach but the rafters had taken over again. I didn't like them much because they stole my swing that was hanging from the ponderosa and floated it off down the river. Anyway, my wife drove our truck down among the hogs. We had a-half-dozen sows that weighted better than 800 pounds and a boar that was bigger. Debbie, that's my wife's name, put some slop in the back of the truck and headed for the beach and the hogs bolted after her. When those rafters saw those hogs stampeding toward them, they grabbed their beer and took off down the river."

"I wish I could have seen that," I say.

"We got the best of them that time," he says as he smiles from ear-to-ear.

I look at his beautiful white-sand beach. It is shaded by a ponderosa and a long scrap-iron swing hangs from a tree that also holds a tree house. "Let them try to float this one away." He laughs again. "I tried to get Debbie to sleep up there in the tree house but she won't do it. She's afraid she'll fall out. No, I couldn't sell this place—it's all I've got," he says.

"This is a gorgeous beach," I say to change the subject.

He talks about the gnarled trees that grow on the hillside without water. "They've been here longer than people."

"What are they called?" I ask as I take a leaf.

"I don't know. We just call them the ancient trees."

I'm in the driver's seat of my car starting the engine and he is hunched against the open window.

"Come back again, anytime, and look around if you want."

"Thank you. I'd like that. Some day I will."

"If you want to see my other beach on your way out, go about a hundred yards passed the Conoco sign and turn toward the river at the cash register." In the rear-view mirror, I see Billy waving goodbye. I toot the horn.

As I cross the iron bridge and head north on Highway 55, I come to a point where I can look across the Payette River just like I always have, but this time I have lost my anger. Why was I so furious with Billy Watson in the first place? It isn't his fault that my grandparents died and things at the ranch aren't like they used to be.

Now, as I drive up the river, I won't just think about my grandparents, I'll think about Billy Watson, as well. I'll look to see if he is running hogs against the river, and I'll stretch my neck to get a good look at his beautiful white sand beach with its big scrap-metal swing under the ponderosa. I'll chuckle when I think about Billy's country humor: the parking meter, the Conoco sign, and the old cash register. I'll check to see if he has buried any of his treasure to dig up later.

And I'll make it a point to identify this leaf so I can tell him the botanical name of his ancient trees. That will give me a reason to return.

TEMPORARILY PERMANENT

Coonrod, a woman who had no sense of style, ran a one-chair beauty parlor in her kitchen a block and a half from our house. Because she was a widow, and because she didn't charge much, my mother occasionally had her do her hair. It was late August and I was about to enter the third grade when mother convinced me how grown up I would look with my first permanent as she marched me down the street to Coonrod's.

I was a skinny little kid with a freckled face, a pug nose and strawberry-blond hair. I liked my hair because my father often said it was spun gold.

Coonrod was a sullen old woman who barely grunted in answer to my endless questions about what she was going to do to me. She sat me in a tall chair and beneath a monstrous machine, much like a torture rack out of a Boris Karloff movie. Giant clamps hung from oversize electric cords like menacing spiders. The very sight of it made me antsy; I wanted to go home. Coonrod slathered a smelly solution on my hair and rolled it up on curling rods.

When you're eight, it's hard to sit still under any conditions, and here I was being tethered by my hair to this terrifying machine unable to move lest I pull it out by the roots. Once my hair was tediously clamped, she turned on the heat and over the stink of ammonia I smelled that awful smell of burning hair. Coonrod gave me *that* Frankenstein glare.

I fidgeted until she finally released me from the machine. Bolting from her house, I ran all the way home and into the bathroom where I could look at the damage in the medicine-cabinet mirror. It was horrible! My hair stood out from my head like steel wool in wiry kinks, Orphan Annie style.

I cried—I was furious—I was ruined. How could that crazy old woman have done this to me? Dousing my head under the faucet didn't make the frizz go away. I couldn't even get a comb through it. Convinced in my heart that I was stuck with this ghastly burnt up mess forever, I sobbed. After all, it was a *permanent*.

OFF THE TOP OF MY HEAD—FROM THE BOTTOM OF MY HEART

Learning to be my mother's daughter took a lifetime. It might have been easier if I could have defined her. But she was a paradox, and I was her naive daughter who thought in terms of black and white.

Bertha could be domineering, generous to a fault, demeaning, judgmental, vindictive, sharp-tongued, strong, aristocratic, controlling, caring, a fighter—a peace maker, a problem causer—a problem solver, hard as steel—soft as velvet, a mover and a shaker, a woman with no sense of organization who got things done. She could add two plus two and get any answer that suited her fancy.

My mother was a woman of style, of genteel continence. She had to stretch to measure 5'4" but she was easily the tallest person in my childhood.

Blessed and flawed with too much sensitivity, I loved and feared her in one breath. Love: not just the intrinsic mother/child love, but love born of wild admiration. Fear: a reflex to protect myself from her unpredictable tongue.

At the turn of the century, as a young girl, she came to Idaho with her pioneer father and mother to homestead on the Payette River above Horseshoe Bend. Along a rugged, mountainous trail, her foot slipped through the stirrup of a make-shift side saddle she was riding and up-ended her. Jagged rock and sagebrush battered her before the horse could be stopped. With no other options, her family set up camp and vigil, not knowing whether she would live or die. But she was a survivor; the years that followed labeled her that way. A hump on the bridge of her nose was a permanent reminder.

Her parents were destined to live off the land and that seemed to ignite my mother's tenacity. Her Scottish father, who saw no purpose in educating girls beyond high school, refused to help her go to college. So she filed for her own homestead when she was old enough, raised cattle, marketed them and went to Brigham Young University on her own dime.

I learned early from her example that I could do anything I set my mind to; her dire need to achieve is in my DNA.

Her determination made her follow the man who would become my father all the way to a Southern California beach where she competed, tooth and nail, with a rival for his heart. She won.

She and my father hadn't been married a year when his father died and his mother came to live with them. As Confucius says, "Two women under one roof equals trouble." There never was a satisfactory solution to this arrangement that lasted for the next twenty years.

As the country sank into the Great Depression, lawyers didn't make much money, so Mother became the second bread-winner, which took her out of the house and away from Grandma and may have been the point. But it also took her away from Daddy, my sister Jane and me. It was like yanking the center pole from under the tent.

She organized a Delphian Study Club in towns all over the state for women who had little education and wanted to better themselves. A survey of liberal arts, it covered literature, philosophy and art history. After days of being away, she would come back dog tired, looking old. Once, on her way home to Boise from Payette, she was so tired she "spaced out" and found herself in Mountain Home.

She volunteered at the WPA and hauled boxes of food to the needy in her long, black Chrysler. She had won the car in an *Idaho Statesman* subscription contest. It looked like it might belong to the Mafia with its chrome-covered tires that sat in fender-wells and a trunk that resembled a huge foot-locker, mounted on a rear carrier. It was so shiny, big, and black, it was downright embarrassing.

Sugar, the grandmother name my oldest son, John, gave her, was active in the American Legion Auxiliary and became State President. She entertained Idaho's famous Senator Borah more than once, and was on a first-name basis with Republican Idaho governors as they came and went in the Statehouse.

A tireless politician, she was known in many circles as Mrs. Republican Party. She was an Idaho Delegate to the National Republican Caucus and escaped the "housewife mold" years before Betty Friedan or Gloria Steinem was born.

Old enough to be my grandmother, she was ill equipped to deal with my teen-age years. I knew what was expected of me and would never do anything to disgrace my parents but I was a flirty sort of gregarious kid, while my sister Jane, five years older, had been shy. I must have come as something of a shock.

It was 1941, and before I had been a teenager very long, two airbases opened nearby. It was enough to alarm any mother. Cute teenage soldiers on every street corner added to Mother's panic and my delight. There were stars in my eyes and music in my dancing feet. For no reason I could understand, she became tempestuous. Often, I ended the harangue by going into the bathroom and slamming the door. With the door closed, I could hear her in the kitchen singing her favorite hymn off-key like you might expect of a religious Edith Bunker.

I met a handsome lieutenant bombardier assigned to B-24s. My parents liked him. I was in love and seventeen when he gave me his wings and asked me to wait for him. He left for the European theater.

The last letter I had from him was about the mission he would soon be flying over Germany, and it came with a letter my mother had written to him, enclosed. She had told him to stop writing to me; I was too young. After that, I received my letters back marked "missing in action." I never quite forgave my mother, but then, she never asked me to.

Sugar was not self-indulgent. It was as if there was something inherently wrong about spending money on herself. One day, she phoned me from The Mode department store. A beautiful mink stole was on sale. She couldn't buy it *just* for herself. However, if I would agree to wear it on occasion, she could justify the expense.

To encourage her, I lied. She looked lovely in the mink and it opened Pandora's box. Now, she needed "things" to wear under it. Before long she was a butterfly, mostly a bright blue butterfly, and the conservative browns and blacks were pushed to the back of her closet.

She was an avid life-long Christian Scientist who never took as much as an aspirin and raised her daughters to do the same.

Chatting with her "churchies" one Sunday morning as they approached a local restaurant, she tripped on the threshold and fell through the window into the foyer. Her newest "butterfly" dress was destroyed. The management asked her to submit to an examination at a hospital but she'd have none of it. By the time I found out about the fiasco, I caught up with her limping along, delivering some Republican pamphlets to a neighbor.

I enticed her to change her mind about an examination, titillating her with the idea that if she did, the insurance company might pay for a new frock. After x-rays which revealed that her knees were badly riddled with arthritis, the doctor took me aside and asked me how long it had been since she had been able to walk. When I told him she had walked into the hospital, he couldn't believe it.

I learned to dread our annual Memorial Day pilgrimage to the cemetery. Mother, Aunt Lyle and I went with a muddle of flowers sloshing in buckets on the floor of the car's back seat. On the way, Mother complained about having lost a plastic bucket. At the cemetery, after much falderal, the flowers were placed on the graves. When the job was done, Mother whooped; she'd found her yellow bucket.

"No. It's not your bucket, it's mine," Aunt Lyle said as she quickly claimed it.

"You're sadly mistaken. I know it's mine." Mother yanked it back. Water flew among the tombstones. They were hilarious; I couldn't help laughing. When they realized they were making a scene, our things were quickly gathered and scurried back to the car. Mother caught up with me to say, "You should never laugh in a cemetery, it isn't respectful." I wanted to ask, "Is it okay to fight?" but I held my tongue. Going home, Aunt Lyle gripped the yellow plastic bucket close and when she got out of the car, it went with her.

Sugar was first licensed as a real estate broker after her seventieth birthday. As her knees weakened she needed someone to climb the stairs and asked for my help. I was worried about trying to work with her but as a dutiful daughter, even though I wasn't the least bit interested in the business, I agreed to get my license. She would hang onto my arm for balance as we walked down the street but was so proud, the minute she saw someone she knew she pushed me away and walked on her own.

As soon as I was licensed she put an ad in the newspaper listing a property she had for sale, and left for California to see my sister. I had no idea what I was doing and of course the phone rang off the hook. I called her for help and finally managed to put a sale together in her absence, but it was nothing short of a nightmare.

Early in my real estate career, while making small talk, I was trying to answer a question a client/friend of ours asked me about market conditions. I reiterated things I had read in our trade publication, nothing more. Mother took the woman aside and said to her, "My daughter doesn't know as much as she thinks she knows." Darn. I didn't think I knew anything. Why was she so demeaning? I was trying to help her out.

Now that I have had a successful real estate career, this client/friend still tells that story to anyone who will listen, thinking it is terribly funny, and I fake a smile through clenched teeth.

Because she was capable of deflating my confidence, I finally came up with a method to steel myself against her tongue with a simple retort: "You don't mean that." It worked. It was as though I had figured out how to derail a fast-moving train. It drove her a little crazy but those were the days she needed me, as the years of requiring a caregiver unfolded. The more her physical strength declined the nicer she became. There were still days she would get downright ornery but that became my private joke because it told me she was feeling stronger and didn't feel so dependent on me.

Aunt Lyle died and left instructions in her will that Mother was to have *nothing* to do with selling her house, or settling her estate. I was mortified when it went on to say that clause also applied to me. I suppose Aunt Lyle thought if I were involved, Mother would be, too. I had tried to be a good niece to this odd little woman, who was never hesitant in asking for favors. How difficult it is when the last word comes from the grave and there can be no rebuttal.

My grandfather, father and uncle were Masons. After they were all in the cemetery, Mother, regretted that she hadn't become an Eastern Star while they were alive, and half-heartedly joined. At one of the first meetings she attended, they gave her a rose for being the oldest member. She was so incensed at their making an issue of her age, she walked out never to return.

In her later years Sugar's face was badly disfigured by skin cancer before she would even consider radiation. Once committed, she worked hard at being the ideal patient. She was ninety when I carted her to the clinic four times a week for treatment. One day, the registrar spoke to me as though Sugar wasn't there, asking who would be financially responsible for her treatment. Sugar's face puffed up like a storm cloud. To avert a scene, I told the registrar that my mother was perfectly capable of handling her own affairs, which she was.

People often lose weight during treatment, but Sugar was determined not to. Although her mouth was raw from the radiation, she sucked down fortified milkshakes and maintained her weight.

At one point, she was almost bedridden and I was bringing her meals and hovering. With a food tray in hand, I put my key in the lock, called out, and searched her house to no avail. My heart sank. Out in the lanai I found her open purse and feared she had been attacked and robbed. I was devastated. By the time I reached the alley, there she was waving from her big pink Buick. Marguerite, her friend, was ill and Sugar had fixed dinner for her. What a kick. I was taking care of Sugar while she was taking care of someone else. The purse? Well, she had opened it to get her keys.

She phoned me long distance from California where she was visiting my sister, and she demanded that I be called out of an important meeting. It really scared me. All she wanted was the names of Governor Smylie's sons. I told her I thought their names were Steve and Bill, but wasn't sure. She didn't say goodbye; fact is, she never said goodbye, she just hung up. I went back to my meeting and in a few minutes, I was called to the phone again. She said, "You're right," and hung up.

She was playing games with herself, checking out her memory. Even at ninety-seven when she died, it was sharp as a tack.

Jack came home from his work in Portland to find the house empty and the phone ringing. It was Sugar on the other end demanding he come at once. Without taking time to get out of his business suit, he did as he was bid. When she opened the door for him, tears were streaming down her cheeks. He'd never seen her cry and he was alarmed until she dragged him into the kitchen where she was grinding a horseradish root. It made his eyes water, too. She said, "You grind for a while."

After she took several falls, we knew she could no longer be alone and during the month of Christmas we remodeled our house so she could live with us. She needed a bedroom, bath, and a sitting area with good light on the same level as the kitchen, and of course, she needed her own phone line. Jack and I did most of the work and were exhausted when we finally moved her in. Dog-tired, we stretched out together in front of the television for the first time in a month. No sooner had I pulled a robe over my legs to cozy in, the phone rang. I didn't want to get up to answer it, but I did. It was Sugar calling us from the bedroom, twenty feet away just testing her telephone.

Recently, we attended the funeral of Governor Robert Symlie, Sugar's friend. As we stood in the reception line, Steve, his son and an Idaho legislator, greeted us. He laughed as he told us how his father had always been amused by my mother, who was a great supporter of Richard Nixon. She had hung a picture of Nixon in her living room even before he was elected president. The Governor watched the picture leave its prominent place to travel further and further down the hall. That was when Bob knew that Nixon was in deep trouble. About the time of Nixon's impeachment, the photo disappeared altogether.

In her final days, she held court with each of her six grandchildren individually, either from her bed or over the phone. One by one, she told them how they should spend their lives. She told them to quit smoking, to work harder, to do more, to be the best they could be. She told them goodbye. But even with that accomplished, she didn't die. Many sunsets drifted across her bed. Once the farewell soliloquy is delivered, isn't the curtain supposed to fall?

The day was gray as I stood over her tiny, shriveled body. The grasp of her hand was like the talons of a frightened bird hanging on for dear life. Between her sagging breasts I could see her heart thumping out of her chest and I knew she was dying. Although her religion had served her well, for an instant I could see panic in her blue eyes. I stood there weak-kneed wondering who would rule the world when she was gone. Painful as her death would be, there was no magic to keep her from her final journey.

Although it was hard to lose her, we never really have. She attends our family gatherings on a regular basis and takes over, as you might expect, as we spin her stories, as we marvel at her outlandish life, her incredible strength; her spirit lives on in all of us.

The challenge of being her daughter was hard work, which is a gift in itself. I am resilient. I am who I am because of that struggle. At her hand, I have learned humility and perseverance. I have learn to winnow the chaff from the wheat and let it blow to the wind. Because of her, I developed a keen sense of humor: the best armor known to mankind.

I see my mother in myself. She is in my head and won't be still. Part of me wants to be like her while the other part of me wants anything but that. Earlier in life, I thought she was like other mothers, but that isn't true. This woman pioneered her way through life, dared to do the unthinkable, broke the feminine mold, and made a deep and lasting impression on her family and all who knew her. She was, in a word, remarkable.

THESE FOOTHILLS

These foothills are a part of my childhood. I know their trails, cervices, and caves. I can still taste the acrid stems of wild onion that bloomed there in spring and envision how the caliche soil cracks when parched by summer heat, sometimes wide enough to wedge a shoe, throw a hiker off-balance, or cause a horse to stumble. I can almost see the raging run-off fill the gullies, those first warm days of spring.

My sure-footed, rambunctious boys ran up these foothills and tumbled down and took their first strides of independence as they disappeared over the rise and it was up to me to let them go. These foothills are a place of lizards, toads, shiny rocks and dreams.

In a cave on top of Beaver Flats, there are petroglyphs that some people believe a Neolithic man carved; no one really knows. From the vantage point of Table Rock, it is glorious to view the far horizon as the setting sun spins its grandeur across the infinite sky.

How many times on the back of a horse, I've seen the town below disappear and the rolling hills become compete in themselves. The stunning lack of man's intrusion gave rise to an inner peace I still call upon. To some the foothills are monotonous, to me, they are divine.

Through the years, we have made frequent visits to the Oregon Coast. As a Scorpio, a water sign, the ocean holds me mesmerized as I walk the miles of beach barefooted, replenishing my spirit, and venture into its bracing water to feel the hard surf hammer my body, to taste the salt. There are never enough evenings to watch the sun dip into the ocean like a blessing.

Yet, on our journey home, the ocean pales in my longing as the first glimpse of the foothills comes into view. They rise like sentinels over our luscious river valley. In August, they are covered with dry grass and as the long rays of the setting sun touch them they become a breathtaking pallet of pastels. It is then I understand the lure salmon must feel as they struggle upstream to return to their beginnings.

TRADITIONS

Family traditions are the backbone of lifelong memories. They are made up of simple details like the oyster stuffing in the Thanksgiving turkey or the cardboard Santa that has shown up on the front lawn every Christmas for the last twenty years. The family that has traditions doesn't have to reinvent itself; it simply pulls out the traditions on cue and everyone smiles their "trad" smiles. It offers relief from the anguish of wondering what should happen next and soothes the tension of family get-togethers. If Christmas is already programmed in the memory bank and once it is dished up, everyone, or at least the traditionalists, are placated and satisfied, then why try to buck this senseless repetition? Holidays are stressful enough without rocking the boat.

Well, I'll tell you why: because the only holidays that are memorable have nothing to do with tradition but rather some odd happening like—that was the year our little black chow, Mauni Rumples, was accidentally left in the car and we spent the entire Christmas day looking for her; or what fun Kris was on his very first Christmas when he was six months old; or the year an electrical storm cut off the power with the turkey half done and we dragged it outside to the barbecue in a foot of snow.

So "tradition" is only a means of muddling through, and it's boring. Why anyone really wants the same old, same old is beyond me. Perhaps there is comfort in the familiar but it certainly isn't very creative. I like to bring some spontaneity to the table, make folks wake up and take notice instead of sleeping through another holiday. I am not happy unless I can do that.

My oldest son, John is a traditionalist. He hates change. He doesn't even like new clothes. Imagine what it has been like for him to have a mother like me. But I can't do anything about it now; it would mean another change that would surely undo him.

His daughter, Korie, takes after him. I realized that when I failed to stuff eggs for a holiday meal and she bawled me out: "Grandma, you're supposed to do the stuffed egg thing." So I bow to that. It's nice when people have favorites and I can honor them. We have smoked turkey on Thanksgiving because I know son Tom prefers it. I substitute veggies and fruit salad for the mashed potatoes, gravy and dressing, but that's okay because all of us are watching the scales anyway.

There is no question that I brought my own child home from the hospital when our youngest, Kevin, was born. He's definitely from my gene pool. When he was a preschooler and one of my friends asked him what we were going to do for Thanksgiving, he replied, "Oh, we've already done that. We did Thanksgiving last year." See, he doesn't like the mindless repetition either.

I must admit, there is a tradition in the making that I don't mind one bit. Kevin's wife Kathi reliably brings a delicious assortment of pies to our holiday gathering.

A friend of mine, a grief counselor, spoke at a meeting of business-women some years ago about tradition and how important it was to all of us—how people count on it. She said it was the glue that holds families together.

Was there something wrong with my family? With no tradition, were we missing our glue? I suddenly began doubting myself. It had been up to me to make the holiday happen, and what if I hadn't done it right all these years?

During the question-and-answer period, I ventured, "My family doesn't really have traditions."

She smiled. "What do you do Christmas?"

"Something different every year—as different as I can make it."

"That, my dear, is your tradition." I guess that means I'm off the hook.

Now, with Christmas once again upon us, I'll figure out what new rabbit I can pull out of the old hat this year as I whip up the raw cranberry relish as I always do. No one particularly likes it, but it's my mother's recipe and brings back my childhood, so I make it every year.

A DAMSEL IN DISTRESS

In the spring of 1943, eight of us piled into a 1937 Ford as we left Boise High School's Spring Prom in our formal gowns and suits. A mélange of arms and legs became so entangled it was hard to know what belonged to whom. High heels and elbows jabbed in vulnerable places. Gowns were wrinkled and hair-dos disheveled, but it didn't matter because the dance was over. After an evening of being proper ladies and gentlemen, we could go back to being the kids we were.

One of us got the bright idea that it would be cool to go to Julia Davis Park and swing in our long gowns in the moonlight. We knew that we weren't supposed to be in the park after dark but that made it all that much more compelling.

Our chiffon and organdy gowns billowed in the air as our dates pushed us high into the night. But then, it became a competition between the fellows and we were propelled to scary heights and our squeals of delight turned to terror. While I was out in space wondering how to put an end to it, a ghastly scream filled the darkness—then another scream and another. That brought the boy's game to an abrupt halt, as they caught the swings and we were chivalrously ushered back to the car with orders to lock the doors while they went to investigate.

All sorts of macabre thoughts went through our heads as our dates crossed the lagoon bridge like the bravest of King Arthur's Knights out to slay the dragon. They disappeared into the darkness and we were left there feeling afraid and vulnerable. After about twenty minutes, they came back and, of course, we wanted to know what happened. They shut us up with tight-lipped cavalier looks as they said almost in unison, "You don't want to know." That left us to imagine the worst: Did they rescue the screaming lady? Did the culprit get away? Was it so awful that they couldn't even *talk* about it?

A few days later, after school, we girls were gathered around our lockers in the hall when we discovered the word was out about our Julia Davis Park midnight escapade. A group of boys were laughing about it and throwing smart-alecky looks our way.

When we pinned them down, they explained, and we finally understood why our dates wouldn't tell us what happened that dark and scary night: the damsel in distress had been a peacock.

DEAR ELM TREE

Look, I appreciate your generous shade on a sweltering summer day, and I'm fully aware that you provide shelter for the song birds and the gray squirrels, but is there some way you could limit your generosity when it comes to your progeny?

An arborist told me you're eighty, maybe even a hundred. That's long past time for menopause. Believe me, I should know. So when, dear, are you going to quit dropping your seeds? I'm truly fond of you, but you could use a little more discretion—enough is enough.

Your seeds come by the zillions, with no provocation—in the slightest breeze they fall, filling the air with pale green snow. They hide in the crevices and instantly sprout. They fill the flower beds with miniature forests; they even grow in the sidewalk cracks. The other trees in my garden, the maple, the linden and the dogwood don't begin to be as invasive as you are.

I rake, I sweep, I blow away your dreams of procreation. I haul your seeds to the trash bin. This week alone, I filled three black plastic bags to the brim with your babies. But no matter: year after year, your unruly teenagers manage to survive. They hang out in the rose bushes protected by thorns. Tenacious, they swipe food I set out for the perennials and invade the beds of delicate flowers: the lilies, the hydrangea and the hibiscus.

Is there no end to your giving? I rake and yank until my hands grow sore. An ocean of hand lotion wouldn't sooth my wounds. Why are you so relentless?

I think of the generation yet to come. I have faith that sooner or later we will learn how to feed the hungry on our planet, that we can find a way to fuse the differences of our diverse cultures as we learn to communicate more effectively; we will become more tolerant of each other, and yes, if we work and pray hard enough, we will achieve world peace. But we can never stop you, giant elm, from dropping your quadrillion seeds, making endless forests that claim every inch of soil.

Some day I will make that inevitable trip to the landfill, after all those biodegradable bags I have sent there through the years have had time to disintegrate, to see the tons of you set free. Your seeds will have grown into forests and spread to every state in the union. Eventually, you will cover the planet and perhaps, beyond that, the wind will carry your descendants out into the galaxy, where, there too, they will root until there will be nothing left anywhere but elms.

A ROAST FOR CHRISTMAS

In the flurry of pulling Christmas dinner together, I stood perplexed in front of the butcher block at Albertson's alongside a horde of strangers, most looking as uncertain as I.

What I want," I told the butcher, "is a beef roast gourmet beautiful to grace my Christmas table. I am thinking of a standing rib roast. You know with the ribs standing all around a chunk of meat with little panties on the tips of the bone." The butcher knitted his eyebrows.

A cute little gray-haired woman gave me the elbow and said, "What you are talking about is a pork roast. I've made a ton of them in my day but I don't have anyone to cook for anymore. Let me tell you how to do it. It was a tradition in our family for years."

"Well, maybe I was envisioning a pork roast yet what I really want is beef."

"I can't fix beef like that, it would be too dry to be good," the butcher said.

"All right. I'll take a rib roast even if it isn't standing. I was suffering from the Christmas crazies and knew I had to get on with it.

"This is an excellent piece of meat." The butcher pointed his knife at a rib roast in the case. "This should feed about twelve. It's choice. Doesn't come cheap," he warned me.

Just then, a distinguished looking man tapped me on the shoulder. "How are you going to cook it?" he wanted to know.

"In the oven?" I asked.

"What you want to do is cook it in sea salt. It will be absolutely the most succulent roast you have ever eaten."

"Salt?" I questioned. All I could think of was how I avoided salt like poison. After all, I have a husband with blood pressure that is off the charts.

The man seemed to read my mind. "You won't get much salt. It just seals in all the juices. Now, I'll tell you exactly how to do it."

The butcher handed me what felt like half a cow. As I lifted it off the counter and dropped it into my shopping cart, my eyes briefly lit on the price tag and I winced. Oh well, I rationalized, this is Christmas dinner we are talking about here.

For the next twenty minutes I took notes as the used-to-be chef explained just how to prepare the roast. We parted after he took me down Aisle 13 to find exactly the right salt. He seemed as comfortable as an old shoe.

"Merry Christmas," I called after him.

"Merry Christmas," he said. You're going to love it. It's the best."

As I put on my apron to settle down to a day in the kitchen, it suddenly hit me that a man I didn't know and would likely never see again, had talked me into doing something mighty peculiar. I'm a seasoned senior and in my gourmet life, I had never heard of cooking beef in two pounds of sea salt. But the die was cast and there was no turning back. The idea of trying something new and out of the ordinary has always appealed to me.

I entertained my guests with peeks into the oven to preview dinner. There were a lot of raised eyebrows, but everybody was pretty much used to my off-the-wall approach to life.

When the roast was done, I lifted it out of the oven, let it cool the prescribed ten minutes and the entire inch-thick jacket of salt lifted off in one piece. The beef—how was it? Superb!

I had a marvelous time telling my guests about the pork-roast lady and then the old chef. It brought all kinds of fun into our Christmas chatter. It was then I realized that such little interludes are what life is all about and I had missed a great opportunity. I could have invited those folks to Christmas dinner.

CARPE DIEM

It was the perfect day to go to Yellow Pine, Idaho. Lick Creek Road, out of McCall, turned from pavement to dirt and narrowed way before we reached the summit. There was Slick Rock off to the left, reminding us of our son Tom's prowess as a climber. Just beyond the turn-off to Crystal Lake, the lush green of ponderosa pine, fir and larch turned into a graveyard—ghostly gray barren trunks and branches bereft of life. Miles of death in every direction, as far as the eye could see, hauntingly surrounded us with the reality of the Blackwell Fire of 1994. Even the willing sun didn't take the shivers away.

Eventually we were beyond the devastation and passed the marker to Ditch Creek, Hum Lake and Cow Creek Trail and crossed a narrow bridge of the Secesh that flows into the South Fork of the Salmon River.

Vaulting pinnacles of rock stretched high into the sky above the river gorge. The yellowed aspen gathered light. Frost had touched the huckleberry and the red twig dogwood with shades of persimmon, burgundy and amber. There, we were delighted to discover one more remote Idaho treasure.

As we entered Yellow pine, a sign in a stump-laden woods read: "Yellow Pine Golf Course"—off-the-wall, back-country humor, I thought. The town was not much more than a single street, a couple of blocks long with a few cottages half-hidden in ponderosa on the hillside. Yellow Pine lost its last grain of verve when Stibnite, a mining town up the road apiece, was closed down in the 1990s for environmental reasons. It had been a major source of antimony and tungsten during World War II.

The inhabitants were hanger-on descendants of Yellow Pine's original population, summer folk who had come out a sense of adventure, and drop-outs from society who came there to "hermitize." We had come in October when the action was dominated by burly hunters in 4-wheelers pulling trailers of every description. Three bar/cafés (more bar … less café) were the major buildings. One of them had a "For Sale" sign out front. The others seemed to be limping along.

The woman running the most promising bar told us she had been caught in a computer industry downsizing and sometime back her husband had inherited the building so here they were. She said she didn't do deep-fat frying or much else for that matter but she could scrape up some micro-waved pizza if we were really hungry.

The bar had indoor plumbing, much to my surprise, and a weekend-carpenter look about it. We drank a glass of wine from one of a line of boxes on the back of the bar, and chatted with a man and woman who wandered in. "During hunting season," the man said, "you'd better watch out for hunters with trucks pulling trailers. They weren't inclined to share the narrow roads. We've had three accidents in one week."

"This is beautiful country, but what do you do to pass the time?" I asked.

"You should come up for a Saturday night," the woman said waving her cigarette. "It gets wild. There's a guy who is really good on a harmonica and there's dancing. The town sort of comes to life."

The woman told us they used to own the bar across the street; they lived in the back. On Sunday morning, after they'd been open until 3 A.M., folks would wander in through their apartment and go make coffee in the bar then come and wake them up. "We used to have a real shake-down at the door to get the crazies to park their guns and knives. A couple of guys were feeling no pain last Saturday night and shot off their guns in the street until they ran out of ammunition."

At the only store, we bought Jack a T-shirt just to help us remember where we'd been and a package of Craisens that we discovered later was far beyond its expiration date. The store keeper was a chatty woman about 40. She told us there were thirty year-round residents and just one child, her eight-year-old daughter, she home-schooled. When they were in Burgdorf, at a gathering the other day, she asked her daughter if she'd like to do what the children up there did and go into McCall to school. Her daughter told her, no. She liked being right here. She thought it was beautiful. "Most of the people around here are retired and it's like she has twenty-eight grandparents. They spoil her rotten. They give her too many presents and I don't know what to do about it."

As we walked back to our Jeep, a little girl skipped across the road, coming our way.

"So, you're the only child in town?" I asked

"Yes, "I am."

"Well, how do you like that?"

"Sometimes I do, sometimes I don't." She screwed up her face in a grimace.

"We just visited with your mother; she seems like a very nice lady."

"She's a witch," she said. With no further adieu, she bounced away leaving us speechless. On the advice of the storekeeper, we took the upper dirt road rather than a paved road to Warm Lake. According to her it was wider and not so scary.

It didn't hold the beauty of our coming but as we negotiated the switchbacks like a roller coaster descending the mountain, we felt the euphoria of having taken a road less traveled.

Yellow Pine—a fragile reminder of yesteryear, tucked in a glorious setting, was like so many other fading elements born of Idaho's pioneer days. Inevitably, old buildings are bound to collapse and disappear from the landscape. Soon there won't be much to remind us what is was like for those gutsy pioneers who traveled on wagon and horseback with the promise of sudden wealth driving them over some of the roughest terrain known to man. All the more reason to go while we can.

NOT BAD BY A DAM SITE

December 23, 1950: The mercury dropped to the downside of twenty below zero. Jack and I drove across the narrow bridge leaving the Flathead River canyon in northern Montana and into uncertain weather, as we headed south. The syncopated rhythm of tire chains and windshield wipers thumping in unison prodded us along in the frigid tomb of a new-to-us 1939 Chevy.

The three feet of snow out the window would likely be five by the time we returned the first week in January. Five hundred miles of frozen, desolate terrain and its questionable roads were all that separated us from Christmas with our families in Boise, Idaho.

This was our first year in Northwest Montana. Hungry Horse Village was crammed between gigantic escarpments where cookie-cutter housing lined the streets with a degree of monotony typical of government villages. The only thing that distinguished our house from the rest was a lovely fir tree alongside the front door. When the snow melted that spring, we discovered it was the last tenant's Christmas tree and there was nothing to do but cut it up for firewood.

The town of Hungry Horse, a wide spot in the road near our village sported a smattering of taverns, a barstool restaurant, a couple of gas stations and a drug store. Below the government camp, General-Shea-Morrison, the construction conglomerate, built a Quonset hut grocery store for the dam workers, our primary food source. Until we finally got a car, we carried our groceries a mile, uphill, rain or shine.

After a year of living there, through a winter, we become savvy to the demands of deep snow and sub-zero temperatures. It gave us enough bravado to think our journey south would be easy but, of course, it didn't quite turn out that way.

The winter before, we had rolled our car going over Santiam Pass in Oregon. My nerves were still a-jangle from that fiasco. Here we were out doing battle with winter roads yet again. The Chevy's heater was unreliable, its tires were retreads and the way was long; only God knows why we were so determined to go. Maybe we both felt a need to escape the confinement of the deep river canyon and the stifling hours of darkness that went with it. The sun struggled until eleven o'clock to climb over West Mountain, only to give up by two in the afternoon.

Jack's first job after getting his degree was with the Bureau of Reclamation. He had a tempting offer to go to White Sands Proving Ground in New Mexico with all the excitement of atomic energy, but he chose the Hungry Horse Dam project in Montana.

A recent veteran from WWII, his choice to be an engineer on a dam site was a noble one. He liked the idea of building a dam to provide electric power, flood control and irrigation to farms, promoting civilization, instead of making nuclear bombs to destroy it.

Winter was a time our engineers played "catch up," conducting endless studies that had to be completed before the demands of the short construction season were upon them again.

For the locals, it was different. All moving, breathing things seemed to hibernate with the bears at first snow and began to do whatever can be done while hovering around a pop-bellied stove to stay warm. In those days, before television, it was drinking, eating, drinking, fighting, listening to the radio, telling stories and drinking. No wonder the women on the project played so much bridge and threw lavish parties, for no apparent reason, all winter long. One woman among us handled her boredom by having a blatant affair, bless her. It kept the rest of us from going mad by giving us something to talk about.

Columbia Falls, situated just beyond the canyon, came and went in fifteen seconds if your car was moving at all. The first time we stopped there was the last time. Jack, Irene Bryant and I were coaxed out into the night with a promise of a movie in Kalispell. Both Irene and I were pregnant and as the blizzard intensified Jack became nervous, so we agreed to forget the movie. But our decision didn't come fast enough. The snow fell heavier and heavier causing a total whiteout and cars were stacked up along the highway for miles; some even slid into the gullies. The canyon road was closed and we were stuck in Columbia Falls, along with a horde of other unfortunates.

Stumbling down the highway through deep snow, we congregated with the other refugees in the only restaurant in town: standing room only. As the hours dragged on, a hamburger sounded like a good idea until we heard that the management was charging twenty-five dollars a pop. Before morning, our chief engineer Clyde Spencer used his big dam equipment to doze out the highway and rescue us. The restaurant had written its own obituary that night. Taking advantage of a bad situation was a taboo not to be ignored by decent folk. The place was boycotted and soon went out of business.

Summer, however brief, was reward enough for enduring the harsh winter. As the snow receded and creeks ran free into the Flathead River, we discovered abrupt opulent mountains covered with bear grass, wild flowers beyond imagination and tangy huckleberries big as marbles.

When we arrived in Hungry Horse in 1949, the Great Northern Railway was still delivering a few elite easterners to Glacier National Park and escorting them from lodge to lodge in quaint red buses. Vacationers in cars were beginning to discover northwest Montana, and no wonder. There was something marvelous about the enormity of mountains bedazzled with snow caps, lush forests and a network of mountain lakes, rivers and creeks, a place where wild animals far outnumbered people and stars shone brighter than anywhere else on the planet.

Our days in Glacier Park were golden. We hiked to mountain lakes, slept under the stars, and cooked over campfires. On the Going-to-the-Sun highway, cars were often stopped by bear begging for food. One morning, after a campsite breakfast, as we drove north, Jack threw a hotcake to Gertie, a cinnamon bear with twin cubs. Before he could get his hand back in the car, he felt her hot breath on it as she scrambled across the road to get the hotcake. With his hand back inside the car, he sat there counting his fingers.

We came from the University of Oregon's congested campus to this solitary wilderness, of sky and mountains that belonged to the deer, the bear, the elk, the moose.

The mélange of people in our village, a decade, or two older—came from all over the world to work on the dam. When we first arrived we found them fascinating yet hardly a substitute for the friends we left behind—our bosom buddies who shared our food, our clothes, our dreams in the tight-fitting commune of a college campus. But before long, the people in our village became family.

Here, our cottage, Number 86, offered few creature comforts. Designed by some southern California architect, with massive windows and no insulation, its only source of heat was an oil stove rigged in the living room. Canned goods on the kitchen shelves froze in early October to thaw out in June. The single-pane windows were etched with indoor frost from November until May. The bedclothes, always dank with cold, often kept me busying myself with household chores until Jack had warmed the bed with his body heat.

One night during our first winter, the temperature dipped to a record of sixty below, and our oil stove shut down. Although the oil couldn't freeze, the tank's connection could. I could see my frosty breath as I struggled out of bed, and when I grabbed the doorknob to go outside, the skin on the palm of my hand stuck to it.

With the furnace running again, we poured a lot of hot coffee into our bodies. It warmed us up, but then we couldn't get back to sleep. Over the radio, we heard a weather report from Moose Jaw, somewhere north of us, saying the temperature hovered at 65 below zero for three days with no relief in sight. We had no burning desire to go there. Why we got the giggles, I'm not sure but I think it had something to do with our victory over the elements, and knowing we were out of danger.

The snow crunched under foot on mild days but as the weather chilled the snow began to squeak. As the pitch of that squeak grew higher, we knew it was time to retreat to the oil stove. One day we ignored the warning and went into the woods to cut down a Christmas tree. Icy temperatures frostbit my toes, plaguing me from then on.

During the construction season, enormous Euclid trucks rumbled up the access road to the dam above our village at four o'clock in the morning. The powerful motors, grinding in low gear made our houses tremble and of course, woke us up. It was too early to get up and too late to go back to sleep and that is why so many babies were born in our village.

While I was receptionist at the Project Headquarters, Clyde Spencer, the Chief Engineer, bemoaned the fact that the man who had won the bid to clear the land for the dam's reservoir, was slow to show up. Because it had to be done during that summer's short construction season—time was of the essence.

Finally, a redheaded man drove up in a red Ferrari convertible, unwound his long legs and stood in a pair of plaid shorts: Red Wixon. The very sight of him made the engineers skeptical but he nonchalantly promised the reservoir would be cleared on schedule. Shortly thereafter, two huge flatbed trucks delivered four monstrous tractors. Two D-8 tractors, the biggest that existed at the time, were interlocked to create what became referred to as the D-16. With two engines and three instead of four tracks, they were unprecedented in the world of heavy construction. A short time later, an eight-foot-diameter steel ball rolled into Hungry Horse on a huge lowboy trailer with two sets of humongous chains attached to it. Red Wixon was ready to clear the land. The two D-16s pulled the eight-foot ball through the forest and trees fell like toothpicks and the job was completed ahead of schedule, much to Spencer's delight.

I can't think of Clyde Spencer without remembering him as the Construction Engineer who couldn't stand noise. The dam site was always deafening with the rumble of heavy machinery, but he insisted the office be kept quiet. Jack was advised in a memo that he made too much noise shuffling down the corridor. Rubber heels might be in order. Jack complied.

As receptionist, I sat near a window that separated the entrance from the rest of the building. Even in this backwoods environment women didn't wear slacks to the office; it was a tailored dress or suit and high-heeled shoes. Something under my desk was snagging—and ruining—my stockings so I got on my hands and knees and crawled under there. The culprit was a dangling wire. I pulled on it but it was well attached so I took a pair of scissors to it.

I had the feeling I was being watched and looked up to see Clyde Spencer glaring at me. He was not happy. Before long, Ruth Walsh, head of the steno-pool, gave me the awful news: the wire I was cutting with my scissors was connected to a buzzer at Mr. Spencer's desk. Every time my scissors touched the wire, the buzzer went off.

Although we had adapted well to living in the boonies, we were anxious to make our escape and spend the holidays with our families and friends in Boise. The Chevy gingerly crept down the road. Jack liked to drive fast but there wasn't one stretch in our journey that allowed for that. As we came out of the canyon, the land unleashed from the confines of the high river canyon and spilled flat as Kansas into farm land through Kalispell and Big Fork. By the time we reached Missoula, it was getting dark. We crept over the high plain above Salmon, Idaho, where deep untrodden snow obliterated all signs of the road. As the car slowed even more, I caught a hint of concern on Jack's face. There were no tire tracks to guide us. Were we on the road or weren't we? Jack stopped the car; we watched the light fade and the wind whip the falling snow.

"I've lost the road," he finally admitted. "This doesn't feel right. What do we do now? We can't just sit here, we'd freeze to death, yet we can't move on either." There was not a road sign, a farmhouse, a distant light, not even a tree. As far as the eye could see, the landscape was flat, white and untouched as a sheet of typing paper.

"What I'd give to see a car," Jack sighed. "Keep a look out." We got out of the car, tromped around in a foot-and-a-half of snow that covered the ground. Kicking the snow away, we tried to get a look at what was beneath it. To our dismay there was no sign of asphalt.

I got in the driver's seat and Jack, stumbling through snow, directed me where to go. At this rate, we'd reach Boise by the Fourth of July. I would have been scared if I'd allowed myself to think.

Jack studied the map. "We can't be too far out of Salmon. If I could just find the damn road …" An hour went by, and then another.

I chided Jack. "It doesn't do to go anywhere with you on a Sunday. Something disastrous always happens. Remember that time in Glacier Park we got lost and couldn't find our way back to our car, or the time the tree fell across the road and we got trapped?"

Jack grinned. "We made our way out of that—we'll get out of this."

Finally, out of the desolate and frigid silence the sweet sound of a motor hummed in our ears. As our eyes searched the darkness, we saw the head lights of a Trailway Bus about a hundred yards off to the left. Jack threw the car in gear and zoomed toward the bus. It was a bumpy ride. The underbelly of the car kept scraping on mysterious objects. The wind was blowing so hard we knew that any tracks the bus made would be gone in seconds.

"Can't let it get away. Got to catch up. Hold on," Jack hollered as he gunned the motor until it roared. "Here we go!"

When the bus driver saw us he seemed to understand our plight and slowed down to let us to catch up with him. Finally, we felt a smoother surface under the wheels and in no time were behind the bus, hugging it all the way into Salmon.

I can't see a Trailway Bus today without thinking about that frigid December night; I can't see a Trailway Bus without throwing the driver a kiss.

THE SMILING DEAD

Ever since I was old enough to read the newspaper, I have been convinced death isn't a bad thing. Just look at all those dead people smiling up from the obituary page every morning. They don't seem to mind it one bit.

Through the ages, death has received a lot of bad press. Many religions are caught up in the "fire and brimstone" mentality where death is a time of harsh judgment, of being scrutinized and found, perhaps, unworthy if you haven't lived your life just right; where you might sit in Purgatory forever or burn in the fiery furnace of Hell. Heaven is only for the virtuous few who have never made a mistake. For others, death is the bitter end, as they believe there is nothing beyond the grave—now *that's* scary.

The truth is we really have no way of knowing what death is like. Yet, I feel sure that death is not the end of us because that would be such a waste of all the knowledge, and yes, wisdom we've accumulated here. There's a good chance that our next life will be an improvement over this one and if we learned anything from all the mistakes we made here, we will enter our next existence a whole lot smarter.

It's just the mystery that makes us anxious. I have great faith in the Divine Creator. Just check out His record. He got sunsets right, didn't He? I'm convinced He knows what He's doing. Since He is in charge of my personal sunset, I have great expectations. Why wouldn't I?

I do worry, however, about the traditional concept of Heaven; the idea of everything being perfect bothers me. Imagine sitting on a cloud in the same white silk robe, day in, day out, eating Angel food cake and listening to harp music—Mendelssohn, perhaps—as you gently flap your wings in time with the music. No one is arguing, there's not a single thing to worry about, earthly struggles are things of the past. No one is telling those off-color jokes that tickle your funny bone. You are too pure for that. There isn't even one dilemma to escape through the horns of. You just sit there in a state of inertia for eternity.

Now, that's my idea of Hell.

IT'S THE PITS

For years now, Jack and I have been making treks up and down the Payette River canyon between Boise and McCall, like yoyos on a string. We used to get frustrated when we were caught in the long line of cars held up by a construction worker who kept us captive with her yellow and black stop sign. We had to turn off our motor and sit in the sweltering heat for at least twenty minutes, too grouchy to talk.

Anymore, this is not a problem. Oh, the road is still torn up for repairs every June and July, but now we stop at the Volcanic Garden Fruit Stand in Horseshoe Bend and buy a big box of ripe cherries from the Emmett Orchards.

Armed with cherries, we are almost anxious to be stopped. We fling our respective car doors open and feast on the delectable cherries. The pits fall, one by one, to the asphalt as we reminisce about what fun it was when we were kids to see who could spit cherry pits the farthest. So … the game is on! Here we are, two senior citizens uncouth as can be, spitting cherry pits into the wind. The game gets even better when we decide to refine the rules and award extra points if either of us can actually hit the other person. Jack is the current champion, but I am rapidly perfecting my technique.

We try hard not to notice who is in the car ahead or behind us since it might be someone we know. So far, we haven't been citied for littering, but if that happens, my defense will be that we are from the Arborist Society and planting cherry orchards to enhance the landscape.

The question remains, are we doing something illegal? I can see the headline now: "Old Folks Arrested for Pit Littering." If we end up in the clink and you come to visit, I ask that if the cherry season is at its peak you bring a basket—now, not too small—of ripe cherries. That will keep me happy. I won't care where I am as I munch on my favorite food in my favorite food group.

My cherry pit-spitting ability is so expert already that with a little more practice I should be able to spit my pits through the bars clean as a whistle. Just think of the points I'll make if I can bull's-eye some unsuspecting guard. That may give rise to yet another charge, like "Assault and Battery." But it's a risk I'm willing to take as I need to be amused until someone comes to bail me out. If it should happen to be you, would you mind bringing along more cherries? Just a few pounds will do. We'll have some *real* fun on the way home.

IN SEARCH OF MAYFIELD

Just who is this cockamamie couple who celebrates wedding anniversaries by seeking out one more old-ball adventure? What sort of clowns would consider it a lark to get on the I-84 Freeway without a destination? But here we are, once more, inventing our day, enamored of the back roads of Idaho, intrigued by a road sign that reads MAYFIELD/ARROWROCK DAM. It conjures up a lovely image—a spring meadow, alive with the pastels of ten million nodding wildflowers.

We take the off-ramp because Jack vaguely remembers a high-school friend who once lived there: Ramsey Thompson. He hasn't seen him since high school, almost seventy years ago. The narrow dirt road snakes through dry sagebrush and washboard ruts rattle our teeth but, for mile after mile, there is no Mayfield. Finally, there stands a house, and another and another set apart by desolate untamed acres. Mayfield? It has to be here some place, if only in the mind of the person who painted the sign on the freeway.

Undaunted, we drive deeper into the rutted terrain, not faltering. If Mayfield has escaped us, there is still Arrowrock Dam. We become anxious as we bump our way further into the desert to a place of coyotes and rattlesnakes. I get an irrepressible feeling we are on the road to Oblivion. But then I tell myself, Arrowrock is just ahead. I can almost smell it. It has to be over the next rise, beyond the next curve or the next.

But, there is nothing but sagebrush. I swallow hard. What if the car dies and these two old people are trapped in this abundance of nothingness? We didn't tell anyone where we were going because we didn't know. We could be lost out here for days … weeks. I begin to panic.

And then, it happens: one more rise, one more curve, and we are back on the I-84 Freeway headed home.

EVERYTHING ESSENTIAL

Out of the blue, my grandson asked me what it was like back in the "olden days" when I was in grade school. That caused me to peel away seven decades and reminisce. My childhood fell in the 1930s, along with the Great Depression. It was a time of penny candy, jacks, marbles, roller skates and Saturday matinees, if we could scrap up a dime.

We lived a mile from downtown in a three-bedroom bungalow. Generous canopies of locusts and catalpa trees shaded our lawn, where I spent hours on the thick grass of summer practicing handstands, cartwheels and back bends. The backyard's mainstay was a pair of blue spruce that had been planted by my father, first on the event of my sister Jane's birth and then mine. A rock fireplace, a forerunner to the barbecue, had been erected in the back corner next to the detached garage as a family project.

A grandparent always lived with us: my father's mother, and my mother's father, in that order, who in turn rocked their days away in the same oak chair.

I shared a bedroom with my older sister, Jane, and a bed as well. Four-and-a-half years younger, I was clearly a thorn in her side. One night she took me down into the clammy, cobwebbed basement in the middle of the night to show me the saw she would use to cut off my appendages if they continued to flail on her side of the mattress. How relieved I was when the twin beds came.

I dressed our calico cat, Cracky, in doll clothes and took him for rides around the block in a baby buggy. I had an imaginary friend I kept in my toy chest. Penelope, a liver and white Springer Spaniel, became part of the family after following Jane home in a rainstorm.

Those were the days before sport clothes: our play clothes were our school clothes nearly worn out. Almost everything I wore was home-made which may sound desirable by today's standards but then, it was a big deal to wear anything "store bought." I wore lisle stockings held up by a garter belt to school. I hated them after being terribly embarrassed when one of them, put in the wash with something red, turned pinkish and didn't match the color of the other. Of course, the other kids made the most if it, chanting: "Red and yellow, catch a fellow."

As for toys, there weren't many—probably a good thing—because we had to use our imaginations to make our own fun. One Christmas, Santa *did* bring me a Deanna Durbin doll. Knowing it was a sacrifice for my parents to do that, I especially treasured it and have it to this day. Although money was scarce, our parents somehow managed to give us dancing and piano lessons.

When I was twelve, I joined the American Legion Junior Drum and Bugle Corp. My heart was set on playing the bugle but before I'd been at it very long, I discovered I simply couldn't march and blow the horn at the same time. The only recourse was to become a drummer.

We played dress-up and made up stories about the characters we'd become. Every spring we crafted May baskets from construction paper, flour-and-water paste, filled them with flowers out of the garden and left them on friends' and teachers' doorsteps. My father salvaged used wrapping paper, string from packages, and cut frames from wood scraps and made kites of every description. He gave them to any kid who wanted one. We were lucky, we had the whole vacant block across the street to fly them.

During the school year, mother would invite my current teacher, to Sunday dinner. It was futile to come home whining about what a teacher did because it landed on deaf ears. It was as though my parents and teachers were of one mind.

We roller skated everywhere, hiked in the foothills, played jacks, hopscotch, jump rope, and dug caves in the vacant block and spent many sultry afternoons swimming in a natural hot water plunge, the Natatorium, just a few blocks away. In the fall we made leaf houses that kept us busy for hours. Our Halloweens were more tricking than treating. We soaped a lot of windows and tipped over more garbage cans than I care to remember. When the snow came, we made the most of it with snowmen, snow forts, and snow balls. My father tied a rope to the back bumper of his car and pulled us on our sled around the polo field.

My mother occasionally invited neighbor-kids in to a taffy pull. Even after soap and water and a hand inspection, some of the crystal white candy turned a dirty gray.

When I was nine, the boy across the alley, Olly, and I had a circus in our yard. I was May West with a paper fan, and a flapper dress with ostrich feathers I found in a basement trunk. My mother's friend stuffed the bodice with a pillow and taught me how to say, "Come up and see me sometime, big boy," just like May West did.

Olly was an organ grinder because his mother had a music box: he made an organ out of an apple box and a broom stick and hid the music box inside. Organ grinders have a monkey on a chain. Olly's monkey was a cute two-year-old neighbor. Neither, Olly nor I could understand why little Brucie's mother was so upset about it. Barbara hung from the trapeze by her knees and did loop-the-loops. Patsy played *Yankee Doodle Dandy* on a comb covered with tissue paper.

We tap danced, sang songs and told jokes. Our music came from an old wind-up Edison phonograph that we hauled out of our basement.

Admission was a penny but if you didn't have one, a piece of shiny glass or a button would do. Our circus made the Idaho Statesman with almost full-page coverage which was unusual in those days.

Chores were part of every day living. Mostly it was doing dishes, dusting, digging dandelions out of the grass, and going to the neighborhood store for mother. I'd wash the jars, peel the peaches and make the simple syrup when it was time to can peaches. I didn't realize until after I was married that there wasn't much more to canning. When I was old enough, I was always more than willing to baby-sit neighborhood children for five cents an hour.

On Saturday night, the family would gather around the radio to listen to: *The Shadow, Amos* and *Andy, I love* a *Mystery* and *One* Man's *Family.* When Sunday morning rolled around, we almost always went to Sunday School.

Between built-in bookcases and "what-not" shelves that separated the living room and dining room, actually the only place free of furniture, I entertained my parents and their friends with my rendition of the Highland fling, a Ginger Roger's tap dance, or a long protracted Longfellow poem I'd learned in elocution class.

Our family ate together every evening around the dining table. Often we lingered for hours after dinner listening to Daddy spin yarns. He told an outlandish tale about a Snake River sturgeon that had been lassoed by a Union Pacific engineer to help pull the train over King Hill—a steep grade in Southern Idaho. We all got a big kick out of it, but even more so when Mother said, "Now, C. J., if you tell that story again, be sure you don't exaggerate."

But wasn't it awful being poor? Well, you know, we never thought we were. I can't remember *ever* feeling deprived. We were too busy with living to worry about it. We went about doing what families do and trusted in the Almighty to be there when we needed Him.

After all, there are *things* money can't buy. Things like the way your daddy purses his lips when he is amused with something you've said, the way the sunset flames outside the dining room window across the western horizon, the way your best friend always chooses *you* to be on her team, the way the crickets and the stars grace the night as you kneel on your bed looking out the open window.

BEYOND WORDS

As much as I would like to tell you about Atlanta, Idaho, there are simply no words. You would have to feel in your bones what it means to go in back of beyond along a narrow, rutted road to earth's edge.

You would have to be willing to stop breathing as the road clings to the high ledge of a river canyon where there's only a hair between you and oblivion. You would have to consider abandoning the soft plush surfaces of your life and accept that this part of Idaho is scarcely more than rock.

You would have to confess how minuscule you are when you stand beneath granite that juts from the canyon bottom to collide with the sky. You might marvel that so many years ago, in a saddle, buckboard, or covered wagon, people discovered this isolated place. You would have to imagine unearthed river doilies gophered up to pile high from placer mining left undone—ugly, unforgiving reminders of the lust for gold that lured the fearless to this spot more than a century and-a-half ago.

To experience Atlanta you would have to think "vertical" like tall pines do. Crank your neck skyward to see the giant sentinel Greyloch Mountain shadow ancient miners' cabins that lie in disarray at its foot. Below, you might see a few new boards, chimney smoke, a chair on a porch, or hear a hammer echo through the wilderness and wonder about the "hanger-ons." What holds them here that won't let go? When they fall asleep under a pale moon and stately pines, how do they stand the quiet?

You may wonder who was born here, who died here, as you tramp through the cemetery's dry grass with its wooden markers where years have erased the names once printed there. You may think about their sorrow and shed a tear when you see so many little graves. Will you feel a lump in your throat as golden aspen ignite in a setting September sun?

Oh, go see for yourself. And if you can learn to walk with ghosts, you'll begin to understand those pioneers who knew hunger, who fought to stay alive through dismal Trinity Mountain winters. You might hear them whispering their stories and if you feel a slight breeze, it might be one of them just drifting by.

CHARMED

Griff, my brother-in-law, is forever saying, "God looks out for the Schooler girls." He's right, too—we are predictably lucky. Somehow, we squeeze out of our mistakes. No matter how busy the street, there is always a parking place in front of our destination. We inherited our mother's uncanny good fortune. It is a mutant chromosome in our genes, a special little verve in our DNA that makes even the worst of situations work out in our favor.

PROOF NO. 1

One January, Jack and I were on our way to South America for a month. We were to fly from Boise to San Francisco to catch a flight destined for Miami. We cooled our heels in the Boise airport for a few hours due to bad weather. Finally, our flight was called and we found ourselves making a rocky pea soup landing into San Francisco, only to discover our connecting flight had taken off without us.

San Francisco was socked in and there would be no more flights out until the front cleared, and that could take days. But, there was one plane at the ready, leaving for Orlando. We didn't give it a second thought; we jumped aboard.

As soon as we were in the air, we realized our luggage was still in the San Francisco airport. We had been told before that luggage is never put aboard an international flight without its owners on the plane. I phoned the Miami airport while we were in the air and told them of our dilemma. The voice on the other end confirmed we would miss our connecting flight out of Miami but could catch a flight the next day to Rio de Janeiro.

Well, how about a helicopter from Orlando to Miami? There wasn't time. What about our luggage? There was no way to track it.

We were treated to hotel lodging and dinner in Orlando by the airline and would board the plane for Miami the next morning. Just in case, we'd check Miami's airport to see if by some fluke the luggage had been put aboard the plane in San Francisco without us. Chances were it was sitting in the San Fran airport gathering dust.

As travelers, we have learned to go with the flow. If you want things like they are at home, stay home. We enjoyed a wonderful day at the Epcot Center. We spent the day wandering through old world villages. Every detail was perfect: the architecture, the music, the costumes and the food.

We arrived in Miami the next morning, feeling grimy, facing the unsettling prospect of living in the same clothes for a month. We checked the luggage terminal and found one small bag. Of course, it was Jack's shirts, nothing of mine made it, wouldn't you know?

We had a serious decision to make. Did we give up and go home or did we board the plane for South America knowing we'd have to live without our luggage for a month? We probably could find a few things along the way.

The excitement of the beaches and the Samba music in Rio, going back to revisit the mystical waterfalls in Iguacu, trekking through eastern Patagonia with its penguins, sailing around the historic Horn, visiting off-the-track places in Chile and most of all, Machu Picchu, a life-long dream, gave us the courage to continue. We checked Jack's one paltry bag and giggled our way aboard. Although we didn't know exactly how, we'd make do.

The topaz sea and the white-sand beaches came into view as we landed. We had lost the day scheduled to see Rio but we had been there before so that was the least of our concerns. Jack went to retrieve his bag while I stood in the immigration line with our papers that said we had never been members of the Nazi Party, that we didn't have criminal records, that we weren't smuggling weapons into Brazil, that we were "touristes."

Jack reappeared pushing a cart full of luggage and wearing an enormous smile. "God looks out for the Schooler girls," he shouted, "our luggage was waiting for us."

"Just think," I answered, "if we'd gone home, our bags would have vacationed in South American without us."

PROOF II

Still caught in a frenzy caused by the predictable, yet unexpected last-minute crisis that plagues us when we leave town, Jack and I found ourselves standing on a pier in San Diego, boarding a cruise ship bound for the Mexico Riviera. The purser held his hand out for our passports as I watched the blood drain from Jack's face. The passports were home on the bedroom dresser.

What to do? After the purser made a lengthy phone call, he came back and said, "Mexico is no place to be without a passport, but if you stay with your group you'll probably be all right. Of course, we can't guarantee it. If you go, it is at your own risk." We nodded at each other and then the purser and scurried up the gangplank.

After several ports-of-call along the way, we found ourselves in Acapulco Bay and we joined our group for a stroll into town. By afternoon we were alone as our friends decided to return to the ship.

In our wandering, we discovered an open-air lounge connected to a hotel by a sky walk. Big enough to hold three or four small tables, it was suspended high in the air on a single pole. Intriguing as it was, when it occurred to us as we sat down at one of the tables that Mexico's building standards aren't the same as ours, and as we felt the entire structure begin to sway—we vamoosed.

The tide was rolling in as we cooled off in the surf and then settled under some palm trees on a white-sand beach. It was hard to put an end to this glorious day, but we had promised our buddies we would meet them for "high tea" around 4:30.

On the way back to the ship, we hiked along between the bay and a park that was walled off from the street. There, much to our surprise, was a ticket booth and a chairlift like you might find at a ski resort. After Jack checked his watch for the time, we decided to buy a ticket and take a quick ride up the park's mountain. But our high school Spanish failed us; we couldn't make the attendant understand what we wanted. She kept shaking her head "no". Our persistence won out. With some obvious reluctance, she sold us a ticket. It was a spectacular ride above and through a dense topical jungle, but when we arrived at the top, the chairlift's motor turned off. It was then we realized the attendant was tying to tell us that the lift was shutting down for the day.

Marooned on top of the mountain with no way to get down except on a precarious-looking slide that was too scary for me, we had no choice but to hike down the steep and rough terrain in our sandals. There was an amusement park off to the left walled off with a chain-link fence. Jack offered to hoist me over it, but then, we remembered we didn't have passports and jumping a fence might flush out the gendarmes. As we reached the bottom of the mountain it was beginning to get dark and to our horror the exit gate was locked. In a panic, we rushed along a path looking for another way out.

In the distance, half hidden in the bushes, a man stood hunched over beating something in the bushes with a club.

Flaying his arms, Jack called out to him. "Hey, come over here. We need your help." If it had been my call, I would have raced off in the opposite direction hoping he wouldn't follow. Surprisingly, the man shuffled in our direction, giving us a nod. In a wild game of charades, we made him understand that we were desperate to exit the park. He motioned for us to follow him through the under-brush and into what seemed like endless darkness; it was a long trek before we reached an open gate. We thanked him profusely and Jack gave him a few dollars for his trouble. I couldn't help but wonder, if Jack hadn't called him out of the bushes would be have mugged us?

Once outside, we discovered we were on the other side of the park and in the Red Light District. Not the best place to be in swim suits; not the best place to be under any condition. We hailed taxis, one after another, but none of them would stop. A man who spoke broken-English explained that taxis wouldn't stop in the area because it was too dangerous. He suggested that we walk a few blocks to the right and hail a cab there. We did and it worked.

As the ship finally came into view, its horn blasted its last farewell and the gangplank was being dismantled. We raced aboard after Jack emptied his pockets over-paying the taxi driver. There, we found our good buddies, Jean and Pat, frantically awaiting our return. Once I realized our odyssey was over, I could get a little scared.

PROOF NO. III

A few years ago, sailing in the Caribbean, Jack and I went ashore on St. John's Island. We wandered into Amsterdam Sauer, a jewelry store, where we saw this ring. We had no intentions of making a major purchase, but Jack liked it *almost* as much as I did. It sparkled its way right out of the showcase and onto my finger.

A unique triangular shape, it was a gorgeous blue, with baguette diamonds down one side. The jeweler told us there were only two tanzanite mines in the world, one in Tanzania, the other in El Salvador, and when they were mined out there would be no more tanzanite.

That evening during shipboard entertainment, as I clapped, I felt something drop on my lap. I looked down to see the stone from my ring. Horrified, I put the two detached pieces back into the box where they would be safe until I got home, feeling lucky that I felt it fall. I called Amsterdam Sauer on St. John's to tell them what had happened. They told me to ship it to them and they would fix it. Months later, it came back repaired.

Soon after that, we were in the Mediterranean. One evening we were watching the shipboard entertainment when the same thing happened to the ring. But this time the stone fell to the floor, and it was close to a miracle that I noticed the empty setting. "Oh, my beautiful ring!" I lamented. But once again I found it, this time beside my foot. I sent it back to St. John's for the second time. They sent me an apology and the ring in jig-time.

We were in Lima, Peru's airport, standing at the counter trying to get our flight confirmed. Placing my hand in front of me on the edge of the counter while I was talking to the agent, I glanced at my ring to discover the stone was out of the setting and wedged precariously on edge. I slipped it off my finger and put it in a safe place in my purse as I caught my breath.

Once home, I took the ring to my local jeweler. He fixed it, or at least thought he did. He told me the shape of the stone caused the difficulty in securing it to the setting.

That fall, we were at the Jazz Festival in Sun Valley. We sat in the crowded Opera House listening to The Jack Daniel's Silver Cornet Jazz Band. As I clapped enthusiastically, I watched the stone fly from my ring.

Oh, good grief, not again. After the performance, a dozen people were down on their hands and knees helping me search for the stone, but to no avail. I was devastated. The manager was very kind. He said when the custodians came in to clean, they would look for it. Fat chance they'd find it, I thought. There was nothing to do but try not to ruin the rest of the festival for my husband and friends, so I suffered in silence.

That evening, while we were relaxing in our condo, a man, knocked at the door and asked for me; he was from "security." There was a grin on his face as he opened his pudgy paw to reveal my stone. I couldn't believe it. I almost kissed him; Jack gave him a good-sized bill. This time the ring went to the New York office of Amsterdam Sauer for a major overhaul. It's been three years since it came back, and the ring is still intact. I like to think, it wants to be mine just as much as I want it to be or it would have disappeared long ago. God looks out for the Schooler girls; there's no doubt about it. It's just one of the many perks of being my mother's daughter. I wonder why I haven't won the lottery.

BLUSH

Once we seasoned seniors are considered over-the-hill, we are allowed to be a little outrageous. It is delicious to be a bit eccentric and colorful. I stirred things up at the paint store today without even trying.

The bright fleshy peach I had chosen for the guest bathroom screamed at me as I brushed a sampling on the wall. However, toned down a smidge, it would be absolutely perfect.

Back at the paint store, I asked the pro to mix only half the pigment into a gallon of base and tone it down with a few drops of blue and a splash of black. Spinning his wheel of colors, he dripped pigment into the can and the mixer rumbled. "You've created a new color," he said over the din. "What do you want to name it?"

"Naked in the Morning," I blurted without hesitation. The young man stood there with his mouth agape as he blushed. His face was a dandy example of the shade I was after.

KILLER GRANDMA

Any kid will tell you that grandparents know everything. Jack and I have enjoyed being placed on such a pedestal by our three grandkids. That is until we took them to the fish farm. In one day, we came tumbling down off our pedestals like Humpty Dumpties and our egos crashed into a million cracked-egg pieces.

Whatever made us want to take them fishing remains a mystery. Neither of us likes the sport. Jack would rather watch wildlife then kill it and standing quietly hour after hour saying nothing doesn't fit my "Type A" personality.

I was in real estate at the time, and had listed a fish farm. The seller invited me to bring my grand kids fishing. I never pass up any excuse to be with them, so off we went. The trout were impressive, well over a foot long and the ponds were stocked so heavily, there were almost more fish than water.

Jaime, 12, Korie, 11 and Kris, 8, led the way with fish poles in hand as we tramped around the pond. Jamie's other grandfather had taken him fishing so Jaime knew more about fishing than the rest of us.

Visions of Brad Pitt, with his easy-flowing cast in *A River Runs Through It* convinced me there was nothing to it. But even though I am well-coordinate, I wasn't quite coordinated enough.

Jaime quickly hooked into a nice fish but with five people casting into a pond all at the same time, only one of the five knowing what he was doing, you can imagine the result. The mishmash of lines had us all in hysterics.

At that moment, Jaime's enormous fish snapped the line and disappeared. That caused all three kids to lose interest. You can't ask children to untangle fish lines. That is what grand-parents are for. The three of them had spotted a swing in an old willow tree and found it more interesting.

But the question remained before us: How do you go to a fish farm and go home empty handed? It just didn't seem right. So we cut line, worked on each pole until it was operational, and called the kids back to the pond. They came but without much enthusiasm.

This time, we decided to take turns. We drew straws and the youngest, Kris, cast his line which immediately snared a bush behind him. While we were trying to get it out of the brambles, Korie decided it was her turn and in a wild maneuver snagged Jack's jeans. Could have been an eye, I thought. So we all removed ourselves while Korie and Kris took turns.

The inevitable happened—their lines crisscrossed, and they abandoned their poles and went back to the swing.

In the meantime, Jaime discovered a barrel of fish food and was having a great time getting the fish to gather wherever he threw it in the water. When he realized he had the pond all to himself, he decided to fish. But he couldn't get a bite. He quickly tired of the exercise and joined the other two.

In a real panic, I looked at Jack. "This is a fish farm. No one ever leaves a *fish farm* without a fish."

"Well, what do you suggest?" he asked.

"*You* fish. It's got to be easy. Just put your line out there. There are a million fish just dying to be caught." Of course, by then the fish weren't biting. They had been well fed by Jaime and disappeared under the tulles.

While we were talking, I became aware of thrashing in the water near my feet. I pulled back some tall grass to see Jaime's fish still trying to rid itself of the hook. Grabbing the net, up to my knees in mud, I took hold of the line with one hand and maneuvered the fish into the mesh. He was a beauty, unquestionably, a meal for our whole troupe.

About that time, Korie came back and her excitement of seeing the fish in the net turned to a wide-eyed look at me as she said, "So, okay, who is going to kill it? Why don't you just put him back?"

"Put him back. No way. We came to catch a fish for dinner," I said.

She screwed up her face as she said, "How are you going to kill it?"

"Don't worry about it. Go tell Kris and Jaime it's time to leave." Somehow, Jack had conveniently disappeared, totting the fishing poles up the path so I was on my own. As soon as Korie was out of sight, I looked at the fish. I didn't have the foggiest idea of what to do next. In desperation, I grabbed its slimy tail and smashed his head against a convenient railroad tie.

It didn't work. I'd have to do it again, harder. It made me queasy, but I had to get the deed done before the kids came back. It was bad enough that their grandma turned out to be a fish murderer—I didn't want them to witness the crime.

I was glad no one brought a camera to see me smashing away, again and again until I was sure the fish was dead. I quickly deposited it in the trunk of the car as I saw the kids coming.

"What did you do with it?" Korie asked. "I want to look." I opened the trunk and the three of them hovered over the corpse. "Poor fish," Korie said. "Grandma killed it."

"It's Jaime's fish. He caught it," I was quick to add.

"Poor fish," Kris said. The forlorn look on the kids faces made me feel like the day had turned into a disaster. When they looked up at me I knew that I would never be "Saint Grandma" again—the person they could count on to rescue them from all harm.

On the ride home, the back seat sobbed with laments for the dead fish which grew into a ghoulish conversation about death. By the time we got home I was wondering if I should just fix macaroni and cheese for dinner and forget the whole thing. But then I thought better of it. As I took the fish out of the trunk, I told my crew, "I don't want to hear any more about dead fish. This is *dinner*."

They hovered near me as I cleaned the fish. Cutting it from head to tail, down its belly, the guts spilled out into the sink. Thank God for the garbage disposal. Then I cut off the head and the kids watched almost without emotion, as it became a piece of meat. Together, we marched it out to the barbecue. Once cooked and placed on a platter, it became dinner.

By George, they ate it. It *was* delicious—we all thought so. Given an opening, Jaime is quick to tell how he caught a fish that was big enough to feed all five of us.

As a grandma, I feel there's nothing wrong with a little illusion; the grandparent myth is right up there with Santa and the Tooth Fairy. On the other hand, although it's painful, there's probably some merit in children discovering that even grandparents are human and have limitations.

Naw, I liked it better up on that pedestal, but there is nothing I can do about it now. We've been caught and are dangling at the end of our lines.

THE RAVAGES OF TIME

As our generation becomes the "golden oldies" the major problem seems to be losing things. It's our keys, our glasses, our purses or wallets in about that order. Jack and I are somewhat immune because what one of us loses the other finds, so I tell anyone that will listen, that between the two of us, we have one good mind. But, after yesterday I will have to quit saying that.

We took our protracted trip out to Costco to load up for Thanksgiving. Buzzing the Costco parking lot, we were elated when a Toyota pulled out not far from the store's entrance and we quickly took the space. I remember remarking, "Good, we're not far from the door," knowing that with the cold and wind chill it would be easier to load our groceries. We spent a good hour picking and choosing and gorging on free samples. When the cart could hold no more, we decided it was time to leave.

A harsh wind blew as we discovered the season's first snow had fallen on the foothills. Shivering in our light jackets, we made our way to the car as Jack pushed the cart and I did the guiding. We approached the area that we both remembered leaving our car but it was nowhere in sight. Fighting with the overloaded cart, Jack retreated to a spot against the building while I tripped up and down the aisles looking for our rig. Then, I got a bright idea: I'd punch the automatic door-lock on my key chain and watch for a tail light to go on.

It *was* a great idea, but nothing happened.

I caught a glimpse of my head in a passing car window; my hair was standing on end. I looked like the Halloween ghost. Still no car, no where.

I checked back with Jack. His lips had turned blue matching his eyes. Quite nicely, I decided not to point this out. "I can't believe the car isn't where we left it," he complained.

"Me either," There was nothing left to do but keep searching. By this time I had memorized every car in that part of the parking lot and the search seemed futile.

As I was wondering how comical I must seem to the other shoppers, with my hair on end and my age showing, a young lady sidled up to me. "Lost your car?

Don't feel bad about it everyone does it. This lot is too big. Can I help you look? What kind of a car is it anyway?"

I kept nodding my head. "Yes, I would be delighted to have help. It's a small silver SUV—a 3X BMW if that means anything."

"Of course," she said and I showed her where the car should have been and wasn't and we went from there.

"This is certainly nice of you. I am getting desperate."

"We'll find it," she assured me. But we didn't. Finally, I realized the lady had given up on me and I was about to do the same.

At that moment, a couple in a red SUV rolled up to me and the young woman asked, "You've lost your car?"

"Yes, I have. I've looked everywhere but it's gone. Jack lost his keys a couple of months ago so now I am having paranoid thoughts that whoever found them followed us out here and drove off with the car."

"Really?"

"Well, no. It's just it doesn't seem to be any place and there's no good explanation."

"If you want to get in our car, we'll drive around the lot and maybe we'll find it." I jumped into the strangers' car without hesitation. I avoided introducing myself remembering how the wind had whipped my hair into a disaster.

After a couple of turns around the lot, I saw Jack talking to the parking lot attendant. We stopped and Jack was even more eager than I to get out of the cold. This time we took in the whole parking lot. It was clear that our rescuers no longer believed we knew where we had parked the car. We were agreeable since it was obvious that it wasn't even close to where we were *sure* we had left it.

Then, by some fluke, in a short aisle that ran perpendicular to the rest of the aisles, ninety degree off, there was our car. No doubt about it, there it was. We had been right about one thing—we weren't far from the store's front door. Our confusion had been exacerbated by the fact that Costco's entrance sat at an odd angle.

We thanked the young couple profusely as we jumped from their car to go retrieve our basket of groceries—if it was still there. Fortunately, the basket was undisturbed and as we loaded the car in the icy wind, I felt warm inside realizing there were still nice strangers in the world who would take a slice out of their day to help a couple of crazed "oldie moldies." Once in the car, we turned on the seat-warmers and headed for home. We weren't a mile from Costco when I discovered I had left my handbag in our rescuers' car. I got a bright idea. We could stop at the first pay phone and I'd call the cell-phone in my purse. The nice young people would hear my purse ring and discover it and we could rendezvous with them and get it back. But that was too easy—my cell had been turned off. As I yammered away about how stupid I was, Jack tried to soothe me with the rationale that anyone nice enough to help us find our car would certainly return my purse.

"Quit whining," he said.

"I'm not whining. I am just complaining."

"Sounds like whining to me." He grinned.

Once home, we unloaded the car and put our groceries away. With that done, I decided I'd see if I had any phone messages—if our rescuers had looked in my purse and tried to call me. The only message was from son Tom. "Hi, Mom. Hear you left your purse at Costco." His tone was a combination of amusement and disgust. "Well, don't worry about it. I'm in Mountain Home and I just got a call on my cell from my next door neighbor and they have your purse and I'll get it from them when I get home. See yah!"

Now Tom was privy to his parents' dementia. There was nothing I could do about that. But how bizarre it was that our good Samaritans just so happened to be Tom's next door neighbors. What are odd of that?

At any rate, I can no longer say that between us, Jack and I have one good mind. But there is a redeeming thing. If it weren't for losing our car and my purse and having such a wild adventure in the Costco parking lot, what a lesson in humility I would have missed and the day would have been nothing worth remembering. That is, if I could …

EPITHANY

One January, on a beautiful summer day in the southern hemisphere, we boarded a vintage train in Cusco, Peru, to travel along the Urubamba River to Machu Picchu.

Some say, life holds one perfect moment; this was mine.

The train rocked down its track as an old rickety train will do in mountainous terrain. The swollen river seemed to dance to the same tempo as it rose and fell spewing towers of whitewater. At that moment, the musical score, "Condorcanqui" came over a loudspeaker. No one told me Roberto Marquez composed this masterpiece while riding on this train but he must have. It so clearly capture the rhythm of the river, the train, and the exotic feeling of the rainforest wedged deep between the cordilleras of the Andes.

I could almost see Roberto as he wiped the cookie crumbs from his dark mustache and put his coffee cup down to write these haunting sounds on the back of a napkin. Writing from his soul as his body sways with the rambling train, he becomes the Urubamba. Flutes trill in treble clef, mellow guitars strum octaves lower; the rounded, full-bodied sounds of jungle drums beat urgently.

It's sad but all such ethereal happenings are momentary. The train tracks ahead were washed out and the music was gone. We were ushered out of the train to face a cloudburst in the back of a cattle truck that slipped and slid its way across rain-saturated earth to a yet smaller train on the other side.

Now, years later, I listen to "Condorcanqui" and I am transported to the Urubamba without even closing my eyes. The music swells as the river does and the train rocks in perfect time as low clouds cling to the escarpment of the Andes far above. And there Roberto sits, looking sublimely satisfied, eating his cookie.

978-0-595-44836-4
0-595-44836-4

www.ingramcontent.com/pod-product-compliance
Lightning Source LLC
Chambersburg PA
CBHW051211050326
40689CB00008B/1269